The life and work of
James Salmon
Architect

1873-1924

Raymond O'Donnell

THE
RUTLAND
PRESS

Author: Raymond O'Donnell
Editorial consultant: David W. Walker
Index and proof reading: Oula Jones

Project management, design, layout, additional photography and
picture scans by The Royal Commission on the Ancient and
Historical Monuments of Scotland

Printed by Burns & Harris, Dundee
Copyright: Raymond O'Donnell

Published with support from The Russell Trust

The Rutland Press
ISBN 1873 190 549
1st published 2003

Cover illustrations (all RCAHMS)

Front: *Right* Municipal Office and Bank, Shore Street, *c.*1900.
Sketch design, possibly for Oban.
Left St Vincent Chambers, 142a-144 St Vincent Street,
Glasgow.

Back: *Top* James Salmon's practice nameplate.
Bottom Glasgow Style watercolour of a house design,
dated 'February 1896'.

James Salmon, 1873-1924. *The Bailie,* 1918.

The life and work of James Salmon Architect, 1873-1924

Raymond O'Donnell

'Architecture is visible history and ... is handed down to us for safe keeping, in trust for future generations.'

Frank Worsdall, *The City That Disappeared* (1981)

CONTENTS

'The architect should be equipped with knowledge of many branches of study and varied kinds of learning ... Let him be educated, skilful with the pencil, instructed in geometry, know much history, have followed the philosophers with attention, understand music, have some knowledge of medicine, know the opinion of the jurists, and be acquainted with astronomy and the theory of the heavens ...'

Vitruvius, *The Ten Books of Architecture*
(Book I, Ch. 1, sections 1-3, trans. M. H. Morgan)

INTRODUCTION

'To say the work of Mr James Salmon ... is strongly impregnated with modern ideas of architectural treatment does not necessarily imply that it is an imitation of the work of others following similar lines ... Whether the architecture be liked or disliked, it is not an echo of other men's work.'
The Studio (1900)

At the turn of the nineteenth century the architectural firm of James Salmon & Son were major contributors to Glasgow's urban fabric and enjoyed unprecedented fame for their work across Britain and Europe. The expressive free spirit within the office was the young James Salmon the third generation of a Glasgow architectural dynasty, who was affectionately referred to as the 'Wee Troot'. His work was seen as being in empathy with 'The Four' and forming part of the story of the Glasgow Style, but like Jessie King, E. A. Taylor, George Walton and George Logan, his designs were also recognised as being individual creations with their own unique spirit. Salmon, as these other talented contemporaries, developed his own highly personal Free Style language and stood apart from the rest. This book, the third in the . Royal Incorporation of Architects in Scotland monograph series on major Scottish architects, tells his story, and through it, provides another significant chapter to Scotland's architectural history.

James Salmon, like his aquatic namesake, has always been a somewhat elusive character. Although popular knowledge of him today is very limited, he is a well-recognised figure to Scottish architectural historians but his details are somewhat clouded in the mists of time. While his buildings are well known and valued for their artistry and craftsmanship, the thread running through them hasn't been thoroughly traced back until now.

I first came across his name in 1976 while leafing through that mainstay of every architecture student's library, Sir Bannister Fletcher's *A History of Architecture.* Here one could read about this apparently little known Scottish architect and his design for the Lion Chambers of 1906, one of the 'remarkable' works of reinforced concrete design in Britain. But that seemed to be it and there appeared to be little else available in print. However, again like his namesake, here and there he 'surfaced'. While there was no major publication dedicated to his work there were other articles and studies.

The originator of these early articles was the renowned Scottish architectural historian Dr David M. Walker, who was the first to publicly record Salmon's work and who introduced the world to the unique Art Nouveau inspired dimension of his designs. Further researchers have expanded Salmon's story. My own tutor at the University of Strathclyde, Dr Frank A. Walker, contributed through his study of Salmon's house designs in Kilmacolm — to my knowledge, the first critique to offer an interpretation of Salmon's design development. Patricia Cusack's in-depth study of the Lion Chambers helped to further highlight the pioneering qualities of this outstanding building, not only in the context of its development of structural technology, but additionally in its exploration of the aesthetic possibilities offered by reinforced concrete construction.

In recent years our particular 'Salmon' has appeared in public more regularly, if perhaps still only fleetingly. Gavin Stamp has acknowledged his unique talent in a European context. My own articles on Salmon for the *C. R. Mackintosh Society Journal*, *Architectural Design* and *The RIBA Journal* have undoubtedly helped to spread the word. But perhaps more importantly the reaction to them has proved that there is a story that needs and deserves to be told.

Since I completed my thesis on Salmon in 1985, more information has been published on Glasgow's turn of the century artists, adding significantly to our understanding of their work, and perhaps adding to the present renaissance in Glasgow's architectural reputation. Almost fatefully this growth in knowledge has also been matched with fresh information on Salmon's life and work emerging in the public realm.

One of the most significant matters to occur has been the acquisition of Salmon's private papers and drawings by the Royal Commission on the Ancient and Historical Monuments of Scotland in Edinburgh. David W. Walker's accompanying catalogue and text to what is now known as the Salmon Collection, has added significantly to our understanding of Salmon's character and the human dimension and interrelationships that prevailed between his business and private lives. David has also woven into his research family information from Salmon's letters to his brother in New Zealand (information generously provided by the Francis family, Hugh Alexander Salmon's remaining relatives). Other information has also emerged from the Worsdall Collection at Glasgow City Archives, revealing telling details about the last years of Salmon's business relationship with his partner John Gaff Gillespie. These developments have collectively ensured that the time is now right for a comprehensive publication to be presented on the life and work of James Salmon.

The following text interrogates what the Glasgow Style actually was and looks beyond the formal and aesthetic similarities prevalent between the artists to consider what they were endeavouring to express and release. Recent writers such as T. Neat and J. Burkhauser have offered fresh interpretations on the spirit of the Glasgow Stylists' designs and revealed numerous layers of meaning that can be found in their work. Salmon is accordingly analyzed in the context of a spiritual movement as opposed to a formally led stylistic genre.

Central to Salmon's early buildings was the influence of European Art Nouveau and the New Art work of sculptors such as Auguste Rodin and Francis Derwent Wood. On the Continent, sculptural forms had gradually become more and more physically integrated into architectural compositions and were no longer 'add-ons'. They were *of* the building as opposed to being *on* the building. Pilasters and lintols merged with their adjacent surfaces, apparently shifting and heaving. The sculptors and other artisans were central figures in this working relationship and a common empathy with the architect-artist's spiritual ambition was essential. In this age the architects were the composers and conductors, with the artisans fulfilling the rôle of musicians. However, just as a musician playing well and accurately to a set score will usurp the symphonic result with the wrong accentuation, so the artisan will produce formal conflict with the slightest shift in proportion, or shortness or elongation of line. Salmon in turn carefully selected, engaged, and coordinated a remarkable array of local and international artists who were sympathetic to his aesthetic ambitions.

A sense of complete unity and linking through art with the universe was also one of his aspirations. Perhaps the Baroque or Rococo periods provide the closest architectural equivalent where *one-ness* with a heavenly world was also an aim. However, Salmon and his fellow Scots had a different philosophical foundation. Their Celtic roots, empathy with nature, and focus on Druidic culture produced a uniquely northern art linked to a universe inspired by the natural world.

At the heart of Salmon's design approach was a strong rationale and methodology, which suffused all of his thinking, writing, and architecture. While his work displays wit, intuition, and touch, there is always close technical and aesthetic control exercised. His buildings traversed between the dusk of the Victorian Age through to the dawning of the Edwardian, moving from the era of traditional load-bearing construction, through the advent of the steel frame and the development of the cantilever, ultimately concluding with the monolithic structural system of reinforced concrete. Driven by his methodical approach he embraced the new scientific opportunities presented in his lifetime and in turn pushed the boundaries of architectural expression further than any other British architect of his generation. Only the contemporary Louis Sullivan in Chicago equalled his vision and technological imagination.

He did not work in isolation however, but in close collaboration with his partner John Gaff Gillespie (founder of Gillespie, Kidd and Coia), and at times it is very difficult to separate the individual contributions they made to the various office projects. An important indicator of their individual realms of influence and responsibility is provided by their Fellowship nomination papers to the Royal Institute of British Architects which they prepared and signed on the same day — presumably in collaboration and agreement. These papers record each partner being accredited with specific projects — a clear split of the office work being established. While the practical reality of developing the projects may not have been as clear-cut as this record implies, it would be fair to assume that one partner would not have let the other claim design credit for work which they themselves had been responsible for — certainly not with such an august body as the RIBA. Accordingly this record has led the attribution of work in the text and hence the critical analysis of the buildings. It is important to note that I have found no conflicting factual evidence to this record and indeed there is substantial circumstantial evidence supporting it — most notably the choice of artisan utilised by each partner for the various projects. Aside from the buildings noted in the RIBA statements, there remains a large corpus of their work that cannot be so readily assigned. We know that they exchanged design ideas and probably worked jointly on various projects. Indeed the late Frank Worsdall felt that many of their buildings showed evidence of Gillespie's hand as opposed to that of Salmon. While I have endeavoured to conclude where I think authorship lies — analysing matters as varied from aesthetic nuances to drawing styles — I have also tried to give voice to areas of debate within the book.

The body of the text is divided into four parts: two main sections, each previewed by two introductory chapters.

The first section provides a biographical account of Salmon's life, which is previewed with a background piece on nineteenth century Glasgow and the existing architectural and artistic scene. In this preview the major exponents and sources of the Glasgow Style are discussed against the background of the work of mainstream figures such as Sir J. J. Burnet, J. A. Campbell and William Leiper, and contemporary movements such as the Glasgow Boys artistic group, the emergence of Art Nouveau in Europe and the Arts and Crafts philosophy championed by Francis Newbery at the Glasgow School of Art. The following chapters of the main section concentrate on Salmon's family life, their Victorian architectural and artistic background, his apprenticeship and development within and outside the office, the years of critical success and decline, and concludes with an account of his work alone. This section also reveals his character and personality, renowned sense of humour, and his commitment to social causes including the Garden City movement. His concern with the holistic nature of architecture, its influence on society as a whole, and particularly on the quality of life of the poorer classes is also examined.

The second section provides in depth discussions of Salmon's major buildings and the design journey he travelled. It is previewed by a discussion of his philosophy in the context of contemporary aesthetic and religious thinking, thereby providing a unique critical basis for the architectural analysis that follows. The second section commences with the development of Salmon's early style, from his Leiper influenced apprenticeship to the technical and sculptural sophistication of the Hatrack, which is examined in-depth in both a Scottish and Continental context. His relationship with Gillespie and the differences between their work provides the basis for an exploration of the variations that the Glasgow Style could embrace — although close companions, their work is quite distinct in both expression and spirit. Salmon's movement away from the free early Glasgow Style work towards simplicity and functionality is next traced in a discussion of his domestic commissions with the increasing evidence of a strong design rationale and methodology emerging. The final chapter of the analysis section is an in depth study of the Lion Chambers. It draws together Salmon's philosophy, architectural methodology, technological awareness, and design rationale and traces through this work the transformation from the Glasgow Style to Modernism and the beginnings of the International Style.

A concluding chapter discusses the relationship between Salmon's work and that of his friends and contemporaries including C. R. Mackintosh. Stylistic similarities and variations are debated in the context of the different aesthetic spirits they expressed and pursued. The historical criticism of Salmon by the German commentator Hermann Muthesius is also considered, particularly his dismissal of Salmon's work at a formal and compositional level, and his failure to explore his philosophical inspiration and systematic aesthetic approach. Finally Salmon and Mackintosh's individual design approaches are examined with particular scrutiny given to their differing responses to the emerging technologies of their time.

Before I commenced studying architecture in 1976, and before I had acquired my copy of Sir Bannister Fletcher's *A History of Architecture*, I didn't realise that I had in fact always been aware of Salmon. A born and bred south-sider I had always been fiercely proud of my home city and its beautiful stone carved pan-European centre. Proud of the buildings that embraced and paid reverence to the classical rules of architectural composition and, as most Glaswegians would always have it, prouder of the others that rejected them, challenged them and dared to be different. On many past occasions I had walked up Hope Street after leaving Central Station and found my attention drawn by two distinctive buildings. One to the west of Hope Street, just a few yards into St Vincent Street, was exceedingly tall and narrow. It had strange 'soft' carved forms and was capped with an even stranger octagonal ogee roof. Also having an unusually large area of glass to its front elevation, at dusk it often appeared to me like a lamp lighting the dark street below. The other building was also tall and narrow but in contrast to the first it was somewhat bare and stark, its white castle-like plainness emphasising a distinguished severity and assuredness. The first was known as 'The Hatrack' the second 'The Lion Chambers'. I didn't know then that these two such different buildings had been designed barely five years apart. I didn't know that the architect for both was the same man, James Salmon. Indeed I didn't know anything about them at all, only that they were buildings that stood apart from the rest.

I think there are many buildings in Glasgow in this situation – they are there, they are different, we all know them, but we often don't have or take the time to find out about them. Then, just as we have the time to look and consider them, assess why they seem to stand apart and make a difference, they become empty, fall into disrepair and are lost. This is a loss not only for the building's owners and users, but perhaps more importantly, for ourselves — because the quality that made them stand out is gone forever. It no longer tells us its story, it no longer makes us stop and look, and it no longer makes us think.

The purpose of this book is perhaps twofold. Firstly to celebrate the life, work, spirit, and genius of James Salmon, and secondly to help raise awareness of his architectural gems that still remain. Many of his buildings are sadly now gone or altered beyond recognition. His British Linen Bank on the south side of Glasgow will soon be lost forever, its Glasgow Style interiors long since ripped out. Unbelievably, despite the fact that technological solutions are readily available, the Lion Chambers still remains under threat. It would be a tragedy if this, or any of Salmon's other remaining buildings, were not saved for future generations. I hope this publication proves informative to those who wish to learn more about Glasgow's architectural heritage. I also hope it assists in ensuring that we don't lose any more of the 'Wee Troot's' masterpieces, because it is through architecture such as his that we not only understand our own history but see our own future.

ACKNOWLEDGEMENTS

The RIAS-Rutland Press, RCAHMS and The Russell Trust for making this book possible.

Professor Frank Walker, and Professor David M. Walker, for their patience, comment and generous sharing of knowledge.

David W. Walker for his historical insight and editorial contribution towards the finalisation of the text.

The late Mr Frank Worsdall for his critical observation and friendship.

Mr David Miller for originally saving the Salmon Collection, and granting ready access to Salmon scholars during his period of 'stewardship'.

The staffs of: Glasgow Mitchell Library Arts & Recreation Dept and Glasgow Room; Glasgow City Archives; Edinburgh Central Library; and Hunterian Art Gallery.

Sebastian Tombs and everyone at RIAS and The Rutland Press.

Rebecca Bailey for patience and support and all the staff of the RCAHMS.

Mrs Anne Francis in New Zealand for granting access and reproduction of information from her archive of Salmon correspondence.

The late Mr Robert Scott Morton, and his sister Mrs Elspeth Hardie.

The late Mrs Mary Newbery Sturrock.

Mr & Mrs H. Lester, Rowantreehill, Mr J. Hamilton of Nether Knockbuckle, and all the owners and occupiers of the various Salmon buildings I have visited over the past 21 years for their assistance and patience.

Thérèse and Fiona for *bon assistance*.

My Mother, Father and Brother for their support.

Susan, Seonaidh, and Euan for enduring, and understanding my pursuit of the 'Wee Troot'.

'This was the age ... of Wilde and Beardsley and Max Beerbohm, of Darwin and Huxley, of Bradlaugh, of Kipling, of the new radicalism with left wing leaders supported by intellectuals' such as Sidney Webb, William Morris, James McNeil Whistler and Bernard Shaw, of scepticism, of licence, of 'perilous triflings with the essential decencies', of feminism, of the Salvation Army, and of the spread of trade unionism. At perhaps no other time had there been such a difference between the points of view of father and son — even more of mother and daughter — as in the gay nineties. And Glasgow was probably at its peak in this decade.'

Charles Oakley, *The Second City* (1976)

BACKGROUND: THE SECOND CITY AND ARCHITECTURE

James Salmon the younger lived and worked in Glasgow during the thriving turn of the century years around 1900, a period of great wealth and development in the city's history. Internationally regarded as the Second City of the British Empire, Glasgow enjoyed an elevated position on the world stage of commerce and communications and grew physically, intellectually and culturally. By the 1890s many major industrial companies had been founded such as James Templeton & Co. (textiles), Walter MacFarlane & Co. (cast iron products), and Weirs of Cathcart (engineering), which all exported their products globally and helped the city became the third busiest British port behind London and Liverpool. The skilled workforces in the shipyards of the Clyde also enjoyed an international reputation for their liners and vessels. During this boom period Glasgow's population grew to be the sixth largest in Europe. Only Paris, London, Berlin, St Petersburg and Vienna could claim more residents! Reliable electricity became more widely available during the 'nineties' and brought with it better street lighting and telephones. Glasgow's citizens also enjoyed a modern underground system. The scientific and medical achievements of William Thomson (later Lord Kelvin) and Joseph Lister drew international attention helping to reinforce the academic reputation of the city's historic university, which had

recently moved to Scott's new buildings on Gilmorehill: Grand Duke Alexis of Russia was famously to refer to Glasgow as 'the centre of intelligence of England (*sic*)'![1] The arts were also flourishing. The Glasgow Institute of Fine Art provided a platform for local talent, while public awareness of the Continental movements in art was ensured through dealers and collectors such as Alexander Reid and Craibe Angus. The work of the contemporary Glasgow Boys group also enjoyed critical acclaim throughout Europe.[2]

As well as home-bred talent, artists from overseas such as the Irish John Lavery, Australian Edward Atkinson Hornel, Dutch Johan Keller, and English Talwin Morris and Francis Derwent Wood, were all attracted to and prospered in the city. Supported and inspired by this background of economic, intellectual and artistic strength it is not surprising to find that the architecture of Glasgow underwent a series of remarkable developments and enjoyed perhaps its greatest period of creativity.

Throughout the nineteenth century Glasgow architects had been in the vanguard of stylistic development. Against the backdrop of the so called 'battle of the styles' between classicists and advocates of the Gothic revival, architects such as David Hamilton, Charles Wilson, Alexander Thomson, and James Sellars, all designed in highly personalised manners, adopting and adapting the styles of past eras, to provide the city with buildings unique in composition and detail. Glaswegian technical innovators

Advert for Walter MacFarlane's iron goods.

Gardner's Warehouse, 36 Jamaica Street, Glasgow, 1855-56 by Robert McConnell and John Baird senior.

St Enoch's Railway Station, St Enoch Square, Glasgow, 1875-79 by James Blair and John Fowler.

also had a major impact on architectural design. In 1855-56 John Baird senior, together with the iron founder Robert McConnell, designed Gardner's Warehouse at 36 Jamaica Street as one of the world's first buildings with both external façades and internal framing constructed of cast and wrought iron. In 1875-79 James Blair and Sir John Fowler (co-designer of the Forth Rail Bridge) erected one of Europe's largest clear-span spaces for St Enoch's railway station, sadly now demolished. As the century drew to a close, Glasgow's architecture also moved on. As in Chicago, where structural developments led to the erection of the first multi-storey office blocks — by William Le Baron Jenney, Daniel Hudson Burnham, Dankmar Adler and Louis Sullivan — so too in Glasgow during the 1890s architects built upwards. In conjunction with the electrical passenger lift, the introduction of steel-framed construction allowed new designs to rise high above the limits imposed by traditional construction and make the most efficient use of the city centre's grid of narrow house plot feus.[3] This led to a progressive change in the city's urban character, skyline and dynamic. Along with these technological developments, two influential schools of design emerged in the city, reflecting two differing philosophies of architecture and perhaps two different generations of practitioners: on the one hand the classicist tradition of expression within an established formal language as

Schlesinger-Meyer Store, Chicago, Illinois, 1899-1904 by Louis Sullivan. *The Architectural Record*, 1904.

embodied in High Edwardian Baroque; and on the other expression through the creation of an entirely new language as manifested in the Glasgow Style.

High Edwardian Baroque was rooted in the exploration of classical forms and orders and the training methods and ideology taught at the École des Beaux-Arts in Paris by Jean Louis Pascal. Sir John James Burnet, one of the most prominent Glasgow architects at the turn of the century, studied with Pascal during the 1870s and like similarly trained American architects returned to his native land with a new vision of architecture. With John Archibald Campbell, his partner of 11 years who was also Pascal-trained, Burnet developed a strong, powerful, vertical style which heralded the soaring refined modernism of the twentieth century, and mirrored the bold compositional forms found in the work of American architects such as McKim Mead & White, Adler &

ATHENÆUM GLASGOW

The Athenaeum, Buchanan Street, Glasgow, 1891-93 by John James Burnet and John Archibald Campbell. *Academy Architecture,* 1893.

McGeoch's Ironmongery Store, West Campbell Street, Glasgow, 1905 by John James Burnet.

Sullivan, and Holabird & Roche.[4] Together Burnet and Campbell designed the highly individual, vertical and asymmetrical Atheneaum Theatre in Buchanan Street, 1891-93, which Burnet followed with the Chicago-like Atlantic Chambers, Hope Street, 1899, and the starkly powerful McGeoch's Ironmongery store, West Campbell Street, 1905 (demolished). The gridded fenestration of the latter particularly revealed his awareness of contemporary American work. Campbell proceeded to exploit the possibilities offered by steel framing on his own account for the design of two major office buildings in St Vincent Street: the Edinburgh Life Assurance Offices of 1904-06, and the forward-looking Northern Insurance Building of 1908. There is a verticality in the handling of both, the lightness of the latter extending to the rear facade where starkly functional wide steel windows sit between narrow glazed brick piers. Writing in 1923 Henry Goodhart-Rendel singled out Burnet as 'the greatest British

The Edinburgh Life Assurance Offices, St Vincent Street, Glasgow, 1904-06 by John Archibald Campbell. *Academy Architecture,* 1904.

architect'[5] of the period, and viewed his rational exploration of the classical language as *the* way forward for architecture.

While renowned historians such as David M. Walker, Ronald MacFadzean and Gavin Stamp have highlighted the variation and achievement possible through the innovative use of conventional historical languages, it must be remembered that style itself is not absolute but remains only a means to expression. Although the High Edwardian Baroque was seen as progressive, its reliance on the formal language of the Renaissance and scholarly detailing predetermined its association with the past and tradition, and while technical developments were exploited in building construction, they appeared to little influence the formal language other than through the scale of the detailing. For all the range of expression possible, Burnet and his generation in turn were not viewed as

'revolutionary' by some of their younger contemporaries, but in fact 'represented order and progress in reaction to the perceived chaotic eclecticism of Victorian and Edwardian architecture'.[6] Historicist styles would not satisfy the up-and-coming generation of architects of the 1890s searching for forms and compositions that would adequately express the *Lebensgefühl* of their epoch. As had been the case with the Glasgow Boys, some of the city's young architects needed to express themselves 'in their own words'. A new non-classical language was required and they looked beyond Renaissance Italy and ancient Rome and Greece for their inspiration.

The climate for change in which the Glasgow Style could flourish had in some sense been pre-prepared by the Glasgow Boys, whose paintings set the scene for a genre concentrating on the spiritual essences rather than the visual impressions of the natural world. They had rejected the sometimes sentimental and narrative style of their predecessors, moving to absorb realism and the purity of form and line found in Japanese art, which in turn led to a tendency towards the simple and abstract. Man and his relationship to nature was also explored. E. A. Hornel's *The Brook* and *Blowing Dandelions,* both 1891, fuse young figures into their environments by merging the patterns of colour with the landscape, the darker tones of the latter adding an atmosphere of mystery. William McTaggart also included children in *Jovie's Neuk,* 1894, and *Christmas Day ,*1898, formally merging them into a tranquil landscape, and linking their innocence to the beauty and spirit of nature. George Henry's arabesque country scene *A Galloway Landscape* of 1889, relies on fluid curves within a flat colour pattern to evoke a restless, natural dynamic from the meandering stream, while David Gauld's slim, elongated and vulnerable figure of *St Agnes,* also 1889, has been interpreted by William Hardie as being symbolic of the presence of spirits upon the earth, with which she harmoniously merges. This affinity with nature also appeared in a prevalent interest and fascination with Celtic myths and legends as illustrated by the totemic wise figures and implied mystical ritual of Hornel and Henry's joint work *The Druids: Bringing in the Mistletoe,* 1889.[7] This expression of a particular northern heritage flourished throughout Scotland. The Celtic inspired magazine *The Evergreen* appeared in Edinburgh in 1895-97, carrying swirling, dynamic illustrations by Robert Burns and the Dundonian artist John Duncan.[8] The emergent art both absorbed this celebration of culture and focussed on the mystical, the symbolic, and indeed the spirituality of life. While the influence and exposure of the young architects to the work and

A Galloway Landscape, 1889 by George Henry.

The Druids: Bringing in the Mistletoe, 1889, by Edward Atkinson Hornel and George Henry.

underlying philosophy of their fellow artists was assured through their studies and educational links with the Glasgow School of Art, personal and business relationships also existed. Mackintosh worked with George Walton (younger brother of E. A.), and was a close friend of Gauld; John Keppie designed Hornel's studio in Kirkcudbright; and William Forrest Salmon, James's father, worked with Gauld in Paisley and was a personal friend of McTaggart and the Glasgow Boys. As the artists endeavoured to express the inner soul and not the outer shell, so Glasgow's designers found themselves abandoning established formal languages and seeking out new means of expressing their spiritual independence. Through the pages of *The Studio* they discovered the formal fluency of Beardsley, Toorop and Schwabe and in turn the Glasgow Stylists also drew inspiration from European Art Nouveau, absorbing and developing the continental language of plastic forms and sinuous lines.[9] Stylistically the molten, merging and re-emerging shapes evident in the work of sculptors such as Lantièri, Carriere and Rodin, was adopted by the Art Nouveau designers who recognised in them an expression for living matter with an inner spirit. The plastic, writhing quality of the metalwork items of Bréant & Coullbaux and the bedroom furniture of Tony Selmersheim are typical of the style. The power of a line also allowed artists to elicit hidden meanings and evoke emotional reactions. Walter Crane was moved to write 'let the designer ...

lean upon the staff of line',[10] and Henri Van de Velde to declare that '*Linie is eine Kraf'* (line is a force).[11] The French illustrator Eugene Grasset also highlighted the dynamic significance of the fluid line, declaring that 'Every curve gives the idea of movement and life'.[12] Such beliefs as these can be seen in the work of many architects of the time, notably Léon Lebègue, and are taken to extremes in the brilliantly idiosyncratic work of Antoni Gaudí. The use of flowers and natural forms also provided a source of formal reference typified in the work of George de Feure. The exponents of Art Nouveau aimed to create entirely harmonised environments and accordingly their creativity extended to all the visual arts. Not only architecture, but jewellery, metalwork, pottery, glassware, textiles, furniture, stained glass, and sculpture all came under the new influence. Architecture, due to its concern with complete environments, was regarded as the perfect medium in which to unite the other arts, and architects came to design furnishings, light-fittings, ironmongery, even cutlery, in order to gel within the architectural envelope. While the new style had many adherents such as Hector Guimard in France, Victor Horta and Henri Van de Velde in Belgium, and Josef Olbrich in Austria, it was not universally embraced. In England the Arts and Crafts movement established itself through the work and writing of William Morris, Philip Webb, Charles Voysey and Charles Robert Ashbee. It was rooted in a somewhat romantic, medieval, vernacular tradition, committed to simplicity in construction without decoration, and accordingly it did not develop the curvilinear finesse of the Scottish or Continental work.

Although never a movement with an ideological credo, in Scotland the Glasgow Style developed its own particular character, distinct and original from other European countries. It shared common ground with continental Art Nouveau in its use of natural forms, elongation of motifs, and manipulation of details, and with the Arts and Crafts in its reliance on the skill of the artisan. However, the use of elegant attenuated curves, Celtic and druidic imagery, and refined sinuous and mystical linear surface ornament, characterised the Glasgow Style distinctly from the French whiplash, Belgian plasticism, Austrian rectilinear style, and simplistic English work.

While work in the Glasgow Style had a very distinctive character, it was not restrictive: it actively encouraged spiritual and artistic freedom. The genre did not suppress the artists' potential for individual expression within a dogmatic framework or restrictive formal language.

Characteristic Glasgow Style pieces are Mackintosh's haunting high-backed chairs of 1897, with their simple tapering lines and symbolic pierced 'nimbus', and his music poster of 1896 with its willowy druidic figure, stylised singing birds, and mystical sun background. This 'other-worldly' quality was mirrored by his wife Margaret Macdonald and her sister Frances in their watercolours, gesso panels and metalwork designs which largely focussed on the spiritual mystery of birth and life. Although lighter in mood, Jessie King's illustrations of this period were also Glasgow Style, for example her bookplates and a leaflet for the 'Arcadian' restaurant which incorporated her innocent, childlike figure, stylised flowers, and delicate curving line tracery, all contrasted against intensely detailed areas. In a different vein again, George Walton's stylised antelope stencil for Miss Cranston's Tearoom in Argyle Street, Glasgow, 1897, has swirling leaf and tendril forms evocative of medieval tapestry, while E. A.Taylor's drawing room scheme of 1901 is in a less rustic mode, utilising elongated organic lines to a frieze and screen, set against a plain light backdrop. A good

Art Nouveau bedroom furniture, 1904, by Tony Selmersheim. *Art ét Decoration,* 1904.

By courtesy of Edinburgh City Libraries

illustration of the haunting, 'spookish' quality of Glasgow Style works is provided by Taylor's dark sideboard for Lord Weir's house. The piece has a central ogee peak and a continuous deep shadowed 'cornice' which elongates to form extended capitals and open 'semi-heart' voids to the flanks. This is contrasted with pierced patterned metal fittings, and elongated oval handles swollen at the peaks and drops. Of the other Glasgow Style artist-craftsmen, mention must be made of the stained glass designers Oscar Paterson and Stephen Adam junior, the furniture designers John Ednie, George Logan, and John Crawford, and Glasgow Girls such as Ann McBeth, Margaret Gilmour and Bessie McNicol.

All flourished in the city and enjoyed international recognition. Inspired by the spirit of the age and artistic energy burning in Glasgow, many local architects were designing with a new-found freedom. Outside of the work of Mackintosh, James Miller designed St Andrews in the East Church, Alexandra Parade, 1904, in an understated Arts and Crafts interpretation of late Perpendicular, incorporating battered towers flanking a central

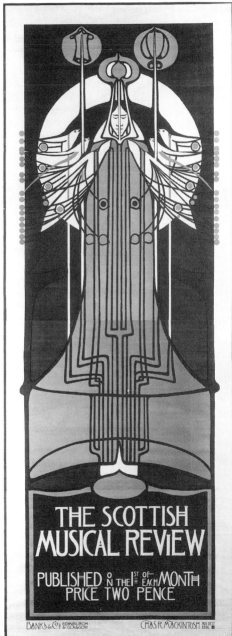

Music poster for the Scottish Musical Review, 1896 by Charles Rennie Mackintosh.

Leaflet design for The Arcadian restaurant by Jessie Marion King.

Warehouse, 118 Howard Street, Glasgow, *c.*1904 by J. Gibb Morton.
Academy Architecture, 1904

The Roost, Glasgow by J. H. Craigie.

Glasgow Style sideboard for Lord Weir's house, by Ernest Archibald Taylor.

© R. O'Donnell

Window detail of Casa Batlló, Barcelona, 1904-06 by Antoni Gaudí.

© R. O'Donnell

Samaritan Hospital for Women, Victoria Road-Copelaw Street, Glasgow, 1894 by Ninian McWhannel and John Rogerson.

arch at the entrance, the total composition being finished with a wide-eaved bell tower. Art Nouveau motifs and a Mannerist approach to the detailing of the stonework were adopted by Ninian McWhannel and John Rogerson for both the Samaritan Women's Hospital, 1894, and Alexandra Parade Public School, 1897. J. Gibb Morton offered simple detailing with a fresh compositional approach for his warehouse at 118 Howard Street, c.1904. He established a rhythmic movement to the upper storey sectional arches which was then played off against the drum of a vertical central tower. James Hoey Craigie borrowed quite closely from continental precedent for his lively public house 'The Roost' c.1900, using sinuous, almost plastic, naturalistic detail forms. By way of contrast, Richard Henderson developed a very personal

craft-oriented approach to construction for his more severe Free Style house designs which were then highlighted with *fin-de-siècle* nuances.[13]

For a few all-too-brief years either side of the new century, the followers of the Glasgow Style flourished and spread their message of a northern spiritual and artistic liberation, which drew international attention to the city. In his own individual manner James Salmon, native Glaswegian and student of the Glasgow School of Art, both contributed to the genre and pushed the frontiers of architectural design into the twentieth century.

'We are as dwarfs mounted on the shoulders of giants, so that we can see more and farther than they; yet not by virtue of the keenness of our eyesight, nor through the tallness of our stature, but because we are raised and borne aloft upon that giant mass.'

Bernard of Chartres

'We are all fellow workers, and architecture is the result of our joint labours.'

William Forrest Salmon, 'The Master Wright and the Architect' (1893)

BIOGRAPHY:
PRE 1888: JAMES SALMON SENIOR AND WILLIAM FORREST SALMON

James Salmon was born in Glasgow on 13 April 1873, and being the small son of a tall father was affectionately nicknamed the 'Wee Troot'. His father William Forrest Salmon (1843-1911) was a second-generation architect of some standing in the city and young James was destined to continue the dynasty and become the third. James' paternal grandfather, whom he was named after, had been born in Glasgow in 1805 and had served his apprenticeship in the office of John Brash, the architect of Blythswood Square, Glasgow. James senior is reputed to have started in practice in 1823, although this would have made him only 18 years of age and

A family portrait of baby James Salmon following his birth in 1873. From left to right: back row, William Forrest Salmon and Hugh Alexander: front row, Helen Salmon (wife of James Salmon senior), Jessie Alexander (wife of Hugh, holding James), and Jessie Salmon (neé Alexander), James' mother.

Courtesy of Mrs Anne Francis

James Salmon senior (1805-1888). *The Bailie,* 1872.

Arthur's Warehouse, 81 Miller Street, Glasgow, designed 1849 by James Salmon Senior.

it is more likely that he began business on his own account in the early 1830s.[1] He was recognised as 'a man of wide interests, a Liberal, a Free Kirker ... a poet',[2] and enjoyed a high profile in Glasgow's architectural and political scenes.[3] He was instrumental in founding both the Glasgow Architectural Society in 1858, being its first vice-President and proposer (seconded by Alexander 'Greek' Thomson (1817-1875)), and the Glasgow Institute of Architects in 1868, becoming its first President (this time assisted by Thomson as vice-President).[4] An active participator in the

business of these bodies alongside men such as Thomson, Charles Wilson (1810-1863) and John Honeyman (1831-1914), he delivered lectures and chaired meetings on various architectural matters. One such discussion at the A.G.M. of 19 October 1869 was in regard to establishing uniform fee levels, a subject ever close to architects' hearts!

In a career spanning approximately 60 years, James senior designed in a range of styles but appears to have been most comfortable in the early Victorian Renaissance of Arthur's Warehouse, 81 Miller Street, Glasgow, 1849. This was his most delicate and refined design and revealed a fine rhythmic, classical sensitivity. He also showed an assured hand in the Perpendicular Gothic St Matthew's Church, Bath Street, 1849 (demolished), the Early English Catholic Apostolic Church, McAslin Street, 1852

Dennistoun as proposed by James Salmon in 1854.

(which was designed in collaboration with A. W. N. Pugin), and Victorian Renaissance again for the Mechanics' Institute, 38 Bath Street, Glasgow, of 1861. In 1860 James senior was elected a city magistrate and gradually became more concerned with municipal affairs than architectural ones. By 1872 he was a favourite after-dinner speaker and had become so prominent on Glasgow's political scene that he was selected as the second subject in *The Bailie's* long running 'Men-You-Know' series. While introducing him to readers as 'a moral man, a grave man, a man of noble sentiments and speech',[5] the article does contain ironic criticism. The author then refers to him as Mr Pecksniff (after the seemingly benevolent hypocrite in Dicken's *Martin Chuzzlewit*) and reflected that 'Perhaps there never was a more moral man ... He was just the person who would have improved the city, and his circumstances, by contriving to enrich it with a suburb [Dennistoun], and to draw the plans himself in order to prevent important work from falling into improper hands ... This is not the character of an ancient Roman, but it is such as we poor moderns are bound to admire'.[6] His *Glasgow Herald* obituary was more generous, referring to him as 'large minded, large hearted',[7] but he was not entirely large-hearted towards his eldest son James, an accountant living in Sydney. Having moved to Australia around 1882, the latter returned to Scotland on holiday in 1887 and told his father that he intended to make Sydney his permanent home. James senior immediately removed his eldest son from his position as an executor of his will and left the nature of payment of his inheritance to the discretion of the remaining trustees. He is thought to have managed his business relationships with equal

William Forrest Salmon (1843-1911).

directness, forming and dissolving partnerships with Robert Black (1800-1869) between 1843 and 1854, and James Ritchie (d.*c.*1909) from *c.*1868 to 1872.

As *The Bailie's* article noted, James senior was not only an architect but also a property developer and estate agent. He was commissioned in 1854 by the banker and merchant Alexander Dennistoun to build a model suburb on a scale to compare with Park Circus, designed by Charles Wilson in 1855. Although financial restrictions led to the project proceeding on a much reduced scale, building work began *c*.1860 and the Salmon family were among the first residents. He also laid out Plantation (Ibrox) for feuing and revised Decimus Burton's designs for Great Western Road in 1859. Other major clients included the Trustees of Hutchesons' Hospital, Paisley Abbey, the Free Church, the British Linen Bank and various school boards. As James senior's commitments in municipal affairs increased, his second son William Forrest Salmon joined him in practice *c*.1866, and gradually took responsibility for running the business with his father's then assistant James Ritchie.

William Forrest was born in Glasgow in 1843, and received his early training from 1857 in the office of James Smith (1808-1863), son-in-law, partner and successor of David Hamilton (1768-1843).[8] In Smith's office William Forrest established lifelong friendships with a number of other talented young men who were soon to rise to prominence: the artist architect William Leiper (1839-1916); William Scott Morton (1840-1903), founder of Scott Morton & Co., the interior decoration and architectural woodwork firm; and the decorative artist James Moyr Smith (*c*.1840-1894/97), who later became part of the ex-patriot group of London Scots associated with James McNeil Whistler and the Aesthetic Movement.[9] The office's main achievements in Glasgow were the McLellan Galleries, 254-90 Sauchiehall Street, 1855, and the original Stirling's Library in Miller Street (finished by Leiper with Robert G. Melvin in 1864 after Smith's death the previous year). On leaving Smith's office William Forrest followed Scott Morton to London, securing a stool in the prestigious office of Sir George Gilbert Scott (1808-1878), and although he later returned to Glasgow the relationship deepened when in 1872 he married Jessie Alexander, sister of Scott Morton's wife Elizabeth. This link also ensured William Forrest retained contact with the London artistic scene.[10] William travelled throughout Europe drawing and sketching, and was recognised as an accomplished artist whose watercolours were said to reveal an eye alive to the spirit and beauty of nature. On his first trip to Italy he was accompanied by Axel Haig (1835-1921), the celebrated architectural draughtsman, 'who as a result became an etcher and a life long friend'.[11] He was also a friend of the internationally renowned painter William McTaggart (1835-1910), the genre and landscape painter Tom Hunt (1855-1929) — who married his sister Helen Russel (1855-1891), herself an artist — and G. G. Anderson (*fl*.1900-1904).[12] The sculptors Richard Ferris (*fl*.1890-1905) and Francis Derwent Wood (1871-1926) received commissions from him and others such as Johan Keller (1863-1944) and Albert Hodge (1875-1918)

owed 'much to his appreciative interest in their art'.[13] He was also a governor of the Glasgow School of Art and became a tutor and examiner in many topics including architecture and modelling.[14] Having been, with his father, a founder member of the Glasgow Institute of Architects, he later became its President from 1892 to 1894.

William's architectural philosophy is not certain, although a paper read to the Master Wrights' Association in 1893 revealed somewhat Christian and Liberal concerns, and a knowledge and sympathy with the writings of John Ruskin. He considered 'that man's earliest efforts at building were the first steps which led him to discover the art of architecture' and the early 'designing men were the master wrights of their day'.[15] He believed the creation of good architecture depended not only on the vision and creativity of the designer but also on the skill of the craftsman executing the work. He regarded all parties contributing to the realisation of a building as equal, noting: 'It matters not whether we be architects, master wrights, or workmen ... All service ranks the same with God, With God whose puppets best and worst are we: there is no last nor first'.[16] He also professed that 'we must not only have honest craftsmen but art craftsmen. It is desirable for your master wrights ... to have art instincts and art knowledge'.[17] In this regard he actively promoted the Glasgow School of Art as capable of providing this training given its high status as a source of art and craft development, and predicted that 'the craftsman who understands and appreciates art will come to the front'.[18] This interest in the crafts extended to his commissioning furniture from Scott Morton & Co., and frieze work from Wylie & Lochead. It is very obvious in the design of Gallowhill, Paisley (1867, demolished), a large and imposing French Gothic house the interiors of which were rich in crafted timberwork, and which were subsequently complemented with fine stained glass by David Gauld (1867-1936).[19]

The partnership became Salmon, Son & Ritchie *c*.1868 and built two major public works: the Deaf and Dumb Institute at Prospecthill, Langside, 1866-68, in a very individual Franco-Italian Gothic style with polychromatic stonework and keyhole windows; and the Middle Free Church (now St George's), Greenock, 1870, in a restrained neo-classical style with round arches and a tall open-crown stone tower. James senior's contacts with the Prison Board also ensured that the office designed the new governor's house at Duke Street Bridewell. The firm not only produced fine buildings but also talented young architects. George Washington Browne (1853-1939), who would become one of

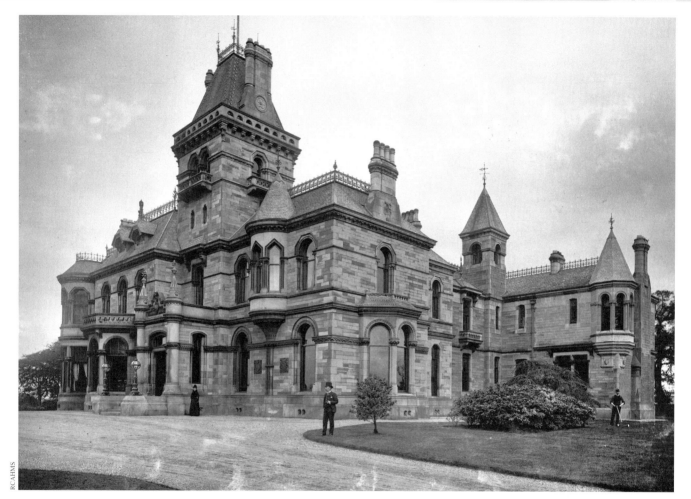

Gallowhill Mansion, Gallowhill, Paisley, built 1867 (Bedford Lemere photograph, 1890).

Edinburgh's most revered architects, and James Marjoribanks MacLaren (1853-1890), the influential Arts and Crafts architect, both trained together in the Salmon office.[20]

Following Ritchie's departure in 1872 the firm became James Salmon & Son, and retained a preference for French detailing and polychromatic effects.[21] They built the Kingston Grain Mills, West Street, Glasgow, 1875-76 (demolished), using red and white brick *Rundbogenstil*, and proposed a flamboyant interpretation of French mansard forms and carved features for the new Glasgow Trades House competition in 1877. During William Forrest's time with Gilbert Scott, ongoing work had included the Gothic St Pancras Station, London, 1865-71, which made extensive use of polychromatic stonework both internally and externally.[22] A series of school designs followed during the 1870s and 1880s that were stylistically unremarkable. The only other works of note were a competition entry for Woodside Church, 1880, and alterations for Allan Glen's School Technical Block at the corner of Cathedral Street and North Hanover Street, Glasgow, 1887-89 (demolished),

The richly carved and decorated interior of Gallowhill Mansion, photographed by Bedford Lemere, 1890.

The Deaf and Dumb Institute, Prospecthill Road, Langside, Glasgow, 1866-68, (now Langside F.E. College).

Middle Free Church, Greenock, 1870 (now St Georges).

the latter again incorporating the office's favoured mansard forms and sculpted figures.

While both James senior and William Forrest achieved considerable standing inside and outside their profession, only in a few instances can their architecture be said to stand apart from that of their contemporaries. It would appear that their talents lay in sound business administration and the professional execution of their duties, and in William Forrest's case, lecturing, tutoring, and promotion of the Glasgow School of Art and its crafts credo.[23]

Details of young James' childhood are not certain but the visits of his father's artist and architect friends to the family home must have influenced his early development. It is known that he

Kingston Grain Mills, West Street, Glasgow, 1875-76.

Extension to Alan Glen's Technical Block, Cathedral Street- North Hanover Street, Glasgow, 1887-89.

Glasgow Trades House competition entry, 1877.

commenced his academic education at the Glasgow High School on 3 September 1883 aged ten, and spent the next five years studying English, Mathematics, Classics, French and Drawing. While he performed well in his written work, it was his graphic ability that revealed a true talent and received recognition in his masters' reports. But as he was nearing the end of his school education the family was hit by tragedy. On the 5 January 1887 Jessie Alexander died suddenly from heart failure while visiting her sister in Edinburgh. James was almost 14 and his younger brother Hugh Alexander was twelve. The loss of their mother must have been a severe blow to the young boys, whose school reports reveal a slight dip in performance. In time, however, they did recover, no doubt helped through their grief by the family, and

perhaps in particular their father's elder sister Wilhelmina.[24] James went on to successfully complete his studies the following year and duly followed the family tradition by pursuing a career in architecture.

'There is always one moment in childhood when the door opens and lets the future in.'

Graham Greene, *The Power and the Glory* (1940)

'Education is an admirable thing, but it is well to remember from time to time that nothing that is worth knowing can be taught.'

Oscar Wilde, 'The Critic as Artist' (1891)

BIOGRAPHY: 1888-1895: YOUTH AND TRAINING

In 1888, the last year of his school studies, James entered the family firm, splitting his time between school in the morning and the drawing office in the afternoon. In September of the same year he took up evening classes at the Glasgow School of Art, attending general classes and training at the joiner's bench where he gained first-hand appreciation and knowledge of the character and uses of the various quality timbers then available to the craftsmen of Glasgow. The head of the Glasgow School of Art at this time was Francis H. Newbery (1853-1946) who, at 31 years of age when appointed, was a comparatively young man to hold such a high position of office. He had trained as an artist at South Kensington and brought a direct knowledge of developments in London and the Continent to the School, and he ultimately moulded it into one of the finest art education centres in Britain. Enjoying the company of his young students, he would arrange for guest speakers to address them, including the leader of the Arts and Crafts movement William Morris (1834-1896). Like Morris, Newbery promoted 'the education of all artists ... [being] ... conducted on one grand principle with one common aim',[1] and significantly he established a broad-based Technical Art Studies course in 1892 which offered tutoring in a whole range of crafts, including metalwork, stained glass, ceramic decoration, wood and stone carving, and furniture and fabric design. Students of architecture therefore spent time participating in other arts activities. The School of Art's prospectus records that: 'Students study ... drawing and modelling (sculpture) from the Antique and Life, and attend ... the lectures on Ornamental Design; Anatomy and Proportion and Figure Design and Decoration'.[2] Robert MacLeod has identified three main constituents in late Victorian architectural ideology which received emphatic attention at Newbery's Glasgow School of Art: the idealisation of Nature after John Ruskin; the emphasis of Labour after William Morris; and a respect for and knowledge of history and architectural historical style. The student of architecture at the school was specifically directed to read Ruskin and Morris as well as Despouys, Viollet-Le-Duc, Gwilt and Gilbert Scott.[3] James's education thus followed the Ruskinian and Morrisian doctrines of the unification of all the arts within architecture, the recognition of nature as *the* source of formal reference, art as a direct expression of labour, and history as a perpetually growing source of learning and example.

On 5 June 1888 James Salmon senior died after falling badly

The Mitchell Library, Cultural and Leisure Services

Francis Newbery (1853-1946). *The Bailie,* 1898.

while walking home from one of his after-dinner speech engagements. This left William Forrest as sole partner of the firm with a significant increase in his business responsibilities now added to the family loss of the previous year. Perhaps in an effort to bring a feminine touch back to domestic life, he remarried in 1889 bringing not only his new bride Agnes Cooper Barry to the family home, but also her much younger sister Charlotte. The marriage was conducted by Agnes's brother the Rev. James Cooper Barry but unfortunately it did not bring domestic calm. Neither of the boys took to Agnes, referring to her as 'Steppy' and their Aunt

Mina also found herself in conflict with the new lady of the house.

While office work appears to have been steady, it was neither bountiful nor prestigious. Possibly identifying a shortfall in his son's chances for development in the family firm through a lack of quality design opportunities at this time, and perhaps in mind of his own rôle as sole breadwinner having to pursue and execute commissions, in 1890 William Forrest sent James to work in the higher profile office of his longtime friend William Leiper. While James had gained second class distinctions for his free-hand drawing and modelling studies at the Art School, he was to suspend his academic education at this time, perhaps due to the pressures of work (and home life?), and concentrate on developing his skills within Leiper's office.

William Leiper, born on 21 May 1839, was one of the most versatile and successful Glasgow architects of the nineteenth century and had particularly close links to William Burges (1827-1881), the Aesthetic Movement and the Anglo-Japanese circle in London. He was recognised as a true artist with a 'keen and critical eye, a fine sense of proportion, a facile pencil and with ... powers of design far above the average'.[4] His clientele was enormously varied, ranging from the local clergy to the Czar of Russia, for whose yacht *Livadia* he designed the décor of the 'Palace portions'.[5] When the City of Glasgow Bank crash occurred in 1878, bringing depression conditions to Glasgow, Leiper 'retired' to the studio of Julien in Paris to study painting. His artistic talents were recognised in 1896 when he was elected to the Royal Scottish Academy and he included in his circle of close friends William McTaggart, and the Glasgow Boys Arthur Melville and Thomas Millie Dow.[6] A free-spirited individual, his architecture was not committed to any one style, ranging from the French Gothic of Camphill-Queen's Park Church, 1878-83, to the Old Scots of Auchenbothie near Kilmacolm, and the Old English of Piersland, Troon. A notable aspect of Leiper's work was the use of top class crafts artists such as Daniel Cottier, Stephen Adam senior, James Guthrie and John Crawford. Within Leiper's office young James is reported to have worked under William James Anderson (1863-1900) who had previously been with James Gillespie of St Andrews, Robert Rowand Anderson and Sir George Washington Browne of Edinburgh, and latterly Thomas Lennox Watson (1850-1920) in Glasgow.[7] A scholar as well as an architect, W. J. Anderson had won the Alexander Thomson Travelling Studentship in 1888 and visited Italy to study. He 'subsequently published the results of his note-taking and sketch making',[8]

William Leiper (1839-1916). *The Builders' Journal and Architectural Record*, 1898.

British Architectural Library, RIBA, London

Piersland House, Craigend Road, Troon, 1898-99 by William Leiper (1839-1916).

© R. O'Donnell

The Citizen Building, 24 St Vincent Place, Glasgow, 1889-90, by Thomas Lennox Watson. *Academy Architecture,* 1893.

which duly became a standard text on Italian Renaissance architecture. At the same time a historian, thinker and innovator, he was a man of high architectural ideals and ability and was very well respected by his fellow architects.

In his obituary, A. N. Paterson wrote 'As a practising architect,

Napier House, 640-46 Govan Road, Glasgow, built 1897-99 by William James Anderson.

as a teacher of art, as a writer concerning it ... Only those who had the opportunity of coming in close touch with him either as co-worker or pupil, could appreciate the value of his work'.[9] He became Director of Architecture at the Glasgow School of Art in 1894, to which 'he devoted himself without stint, learned photography that he might furnish himself with slides that he felt his lectures required for illustrations, and, besides teaching, supervising, and lecturing, personally conducted his students during the Easter and other holidays on excursions'.[10] He also experimented with concrete (without designed reinforcement) in his Orient Boarding House, McPhater Street, Glasgow, 1895, and Napier House, 640-46 Govan Road, Glasgow, 1897-99.[11] There can be little doubt that he must have exerted an important influence on young James. The principal buildings being designed and constructed in Leiper's office during James's apprenticeship were the François Premier Sun Life Insurance Offices, 1889-94, at the south-west corner of Renfield and West Regent Streets, Glasgow, and the *tour de force* Templeton's Carpet Factory, 1889-92, adjacent to Glasgow Green. The Sun Life Insurance Office is a high profile and assured composition that displays rich variation in its stone detailing. Six storeys high plus an attic it incorporates an octagonal dome crowning the corner bay, gable ends, intricate carved dormers, and stone pilasters rising the full height of the corner bay windows. There are sculptured figures to the street elevations, those to Renfield Street being based on Michaelangelo's figures on the tomb of Giuliano de Medici in Florence. Internally elaborate marble sculpture, linings, and timber paneling, all create a rich impression. It was awarded the Silver Medal at the Paris Exhibition of 1900 and is said to have been drawn and detailed by Anderson (see endnote[7]). Such an important commission would have demanded the attention of most of the office workforce and exposed young James to the full range of Leiper's artistry.

Templeton's Carpet Factory was equally high profile, but was a far more dazzling and vibrant building due to the polychromatic brick and tile treatment of the façade. A free imitation of the Doge's Palace in Venice, W. H. McNab[12] spoke of it as 'in point of design and as a piece of architecture and specimen of decorative brickwork, nothing finer is to be found outside Italy'.[13] There is a marvelous sense of *joie de vivre* in the freedom of the coloured brick patterning. Perhaps it could be viewed as an architectural representation of a needle-point carpet picture of the Doge's Palace. The two buildings demonstrate Leiper's talent for interpreting historical precedent afresh, and illustrate the breadth of imagination in his office and the richness and quality of work in which James was participating.

In the autumn of 1893 James resumed his part-time studies at the School of Art and following his 21st birthday in 1894, apparently inheriting his father's appetite for travel, he embarked on a Continental study tour. From April to July he travelled across northern Italy, sketching and recording details from Pisa to Venice, and also took time to venture to Lucerne in Switzerland. On his return to Glasgow he re-enrolled at the Art School in the autumn to complete his final year of study, interestingly coinciding with the session when W. J. Anderson took over as Director of Architecture at the School. He completed his studies in 1895 and rejoined his father's architectural practice in the spring of the same year.[14]

James's younger brother Hugh had also commenced studying architecture in the family firm but he decided early on that his future lay elsewhere. Born in 1874 he was different from James in physique and character. Tall like his father and grandfather, he was athletic, temperate, and had a love of horses, fishing and outdoor life. In 1894 he decided to leave the family home and work for his

Sun Life Assurance Building, West Regent Street-Renfield Street Glasgow, built 1889-94 by William Leiper — reputedly detailed by W. J. Anderson.

Opposite page:
Modelled on the Doge's Palace in Venice, William Leiper's Templeton's Carpet Factory, built 1889-92.

Watercolour study of tower adjoining S. Niceola, Pisa from Salmon's Italian tour of 1894.

Hugh Alexander Salmon (1874-1960), of James' younger brother photographed in 1924.

maternal grandfather (after whom he was named) at Arrat Mill, Brechin, leaving the family tensions at home behind.

While James was apprenticed to Leiper, a young designer, John Gaff Gillespie, joined William Forrest Salmon in 1891. Born on 17 September 1870 the son of a Gorbals baker, Gillespie had served a five-year apprenticeship in the office of James Milne Monro (1840-1921) and trained at the Glasgow School of Art. Blessed with a natural talent for architecture, he won prizes for design, modelling (sculpture), drawing and sketching, and shared the Glasgow Institute of Architects' prize in 1889 with Mackintosh. William Forrest Salmon, an examiner and tutor at the School, had not failed to note this early brilliance and found a place for Gillespie in the practice. In 1893 the firm produced an unorthodox Flemish inspired design for the new offices of the Scottish Temperance League, 106-108 Hope Street, Glasgow and the following year a distinctive asymmetrical composition for the British Linen Company Bank, High Street, Glasgow, 1894-96. These buildings marked a complete departure from the firm's previous work and are evidence of the immediate impact Gillespie had on its output.

As noted earlier, the beginning of the 1890s heralded changes in Glasgow's artistic and architectural persona. The years 1891 to 1893 saw Mackintosh presenting his first lectures on architecture to the Glasgow Architectural Association and his rise to prominence from gifted student to practitioner. William Forrest, addressing a dinner in 1893, revealed his awareness of this time of change announcing:

'At the present time there exists a strong tendency to advance in architectural development. A spirit of dissatisfaction with the later productions is everywhere manifesting itself, and a true appreciation of what architecture is appears to be taking possession of a thoughtful section of the public. Those practising architecture have become aware that it will not suffice to plan a building, and then clothe its nakedness in the architectural details of a Greek temple or a Gothic cathedral, but that each building must be a living expression of its own uses. If it is to exist as an abiding work of art, it must tell its story not only to its own generation, but to the generations following'.[15]

The changes for James Salmon & Son accelerated with the return of young James and the 'spirit of dissatisfaction' dispelled as the forces of change were unleashed.[16]

'It is only with the heart that one can rightly see; what is essential is invisible to the eye.'

Antoine de Saint-Exupéry, *The Little Prince* (1944)

BIOGRAPHY: 1895-1913: RISE AND FALL

From 1895 onwards the work of the practice adopted a radically different character as James Salmon junior and John Gaff Gillespie assumed greater design responsibility. Although quite different in character and physique, James small, bearded, outspoken and humorous, and John tall, clean shaven, quiet and serious, their personal qualities and artistic talents were brought together and balanced by the worldly experience of William Forrest Salmon.[1] James's first major job on returning to the family firm was the design and construction of the massive new city centre office block, the Mercantile Chambers at 39-69 Bothwell Street, Glasgow, 1896-98. This may appear somewhat strange since Gillespie was the more experienced designer and had become a qualified architect the previous year. He was, however, extremely busy at this time being committed to the design of the Marine Hotel, Troon, the British Linen Bank at Govan Cross, Glasgow, and the extension to the West of Scotland Convalescent Homes, Dunoon. It is also possible that confirmation to begin design development of the Mercantile Chambers in fact provided the catalyst for young James to be recalled to the firm. The building would provide the 'Wee Troot' with his first opportunity to make a significant architectural statement, and marks the beginning of his unique contribution to Glasgow's urban scene.

The Mercantile Chambers demonstrated the influence of Leiper on young James, but additionally revealed his own knowledge of London Art Nouveau in the building's sculptural touches. By contrast, Gillespie's Marine Hotel of the same period was far simpler and more akin to the English Arts and Crafts style. Following their High Street branch commission, the British Linen Bank instructed the firm to execute a further two buildings. At Govan Cross, 1897, Gillespie incorporated external Art Nouveau carved features within an overall simple composition. At Main St, Gorbals, 1899, Salmon created a very fine atmospheric Glasgow Style interior — despite the exterior of the project being affected by cutbacks. Gillespie maintained his plain approach for St Andrews Free Church Halls, 1898-99, adopting Late Gothic with subtle carved touches, rather similar in spirit to that utilised by his former Art School colleague C. R. Mackintosh at Ruchill Church Hall of the same period. Salmon, however, was to take the Glasgow Style to a new level with his design for the St Vincent Chambers, St Vincent Street, 1898-99. On an extremely narrow and restricted site he pushed architectural expression to the limits. He married New Art sculpture from the Continent with the developing possibilities offered by steel frame construction, and produced a building closer to the spirit of European Art Nouveau than that seen anywhere else in Britain. It drew considerable attention to the office and generated both complimentary and critical comment. It is suffice to say that four years after James's return to the family firm their buildings were being discussed across Europe — the French arts journal *L'Art Décoratif* specifically dedicating five pages to their work in the golden year of 1899. William Forrest recognised the contributions being made

Mercantile Chambers, 53 Bothwell Street, Glasgow, built 1896-98.

© R. O'Donnell

The British Linen Bank, Govan Cross, Glasgow, built 1897.

Sculptural detailing to window, St Vincent Chambers, 142a-144 St Vincent Street, Glasgow, built 1898-99.

by his two *protégés* and made them both partners: Gillespie in 1897, and James in 1898.

As the new century commenced the firm initially continued to attract commissions, but trends had begun to change. Extensions and alterations to the Marine Hotel, 1900-02, displayed Glasgow Style traits not evident in the original building. Interior work at 22 Park Circus, 1900-04, and 14-15 Woodlands Terrace, 1902, confirmed Salmon's Art Nouveau sympathies and abilities — and also the firm's engagement of artists of international standing to execute their designs. Gillespie continued his understated approach at 12 University Gardens, 1900, choosing only to highlight isolated interior details — albeit again of a very high quality. Although his Lloyd Morris Congregational Church, 1901, was again interpreted from Late Gothic, subtle carved details and

the compositional influence of Mackintosh identified it as distinctively Glasgow Style. Their Glasgow Savings Bank, Anderston Cross, 1899-1900, again featured outstanding carved detailing but here in a less integrated manner than previously. A growing rationality had begun to develop in their work. A Boys Home designed for the Deaf and Dumb Institute, Prospecthill, 1901, was plain in the extreme. Lanfine Cottage Hospital, Kirkintilloch, and the Pathological Unit and Nurses Quarters, Woodilee Asylum, Lenzie, both 1904, continued the trend. A series of house designs gradually became more geometrically focused and the sculptural subtleties of the earlier bank and office work gradually disappeared. The ultimate expression of this rationalisation was confirmed in the design of the Lion Chambers,

Arts and Crafts simplicity of 12 University Gardens, Glasgow, 1900.

Glasgow Savings Bank, 752-56 Argyle Street, Anderston Cross, Glasgow, 1899-1900.

Hope Street, 1904-07. Again faced with a very restricted site, Salmon demonstrated his ability to resolve seemingly insurmountable conflicts between brief and site, and exploit to the fullest all that modern technology had to offer. The design is considered one of the pioneering works of reinforced concrete construction in Britain.

With business buoyant the practice had moved into the Mercantile Chambers on its completion and not long thereafter Forrest Salmon purchased a plot of land for a new villa in the then expanding village of Kilmacolm. Designed by James, again with references to Leiper, the family moved into their new house 'Rowantreehill', in 1898. If there had been a faint hope that Hugh would return home from Brechin at some future date, it was to be dashed when he decided to emigrate and moved to Dunedin, New Zealand the same year. Although now on different sides of the globe James and Hugh remained in steady contact throughout the following years writing regularly with their business and family news.

Their Aunt Mina had moved to a house called 'Gowandean' — named after her father's pastoral poem — in Lochgoilhead, Argyll in 1887. In 1898 the firm designed her local village hall in a very plain Arts and Crafts style — white roughcast walls incorporating black stained timber framing. It was capped with a wide oversailing slate roof incorporating a lead finial cap with a signatory 'salmon' leaping through a hoop.

As the firm progressed, James' profile also rose and his opinions were gradually heard. He had become an office bearer for the Glasgow Architectural Association in 1896 and read his first paper entitled 'Architects — Their Relaxation' the same year, to an invited audience. The paper revealed his belief that while everyone needed time to relax, the architect in his relaxation should be absorbing and participating in all of life's experiences, both at work and at leisure, to enhance his understanding of humanity's need for and use of space.[2] Salmon also revealed his acute sense of humour. He recounted the improvisatory abilities of architectural assistants in devising games that could be played in offices depending on the particular office layout. In William Leiper's office it was a 'crude sort of shinty'.[3] The ball was a sample brick, one goal was the fire place in the ante room and the other goal was the fireplace in the public office; presumably not when clients were visiting! In Clarke & Bell's East End office one could enjoy a good game of golf, Salmon's great love. He particularly noted that 'a dangerous hazard in the shape of a lath and standard partition, blocks your first drive. This is now disappearing, and one should, with good sound play, reach the green in three!'.[4] Turning his attention to church design, the 'Wee Troot' was rather drier in his humour, remarking that 'If an architect is to preserve in his church any suggestion of holy worship, or to aid by his work any feeling of reverence, the less he knows of modern churchgoers and the less he yields to their demands the better'.[5] But he also noted that 'when you think, however, that it is almost compulsory for many to attend church, it should be your desire to mitigate their suffering by beauty combined with comfort'.[6] While it is doubtful if this observation would have been received very sympathetically at home, Salmon's irreverence and sense of fun endeared him to many and his friends held him in genuine affection.[7] When the firm became Salmon & Son & Gillespie in 1903, he sent a letter to Hugh which included a cartoon sketch exaggerating the relative physical proportions of each partner. He superimposed 'S & Son & G' on the figures, giving himself a much broader brimmed hat to make up for his lack of height.

Behind the impishness, however, lay a sharp intellect. He fiercely protested against outdated conventions, loathed pomposity and sham, and was not afraid to express his objection towards the blind following of fashion, and the authority of 'expert' opinion. He had an integrity for truth and honesty, and a natural sense of fair play which led to his involvement in many causes, chief among them being social injustices. This social conscience was first revealed in an article he wrote regarding 'Young Age Pensions' the basic principles of which came into being in the form of child benefits and family income support.[8] His concern for the plight of the less well-off in society was fostered by his friendship with Dr James Devon, a highly regarded Glasgow social reformer who had become the Surgeon to H.M. Duke Street Prison in 1895 (with which the firm had retained links since executing the new governor's house in 1871). Born in 1866 in the City's East End, Dr Devon was 'the fourth generation of Glasgow-born working people'.[9] After leaving school at the age of ten with no qualifications, he worked in a factor's office, a mill, an iron foundry, and an instrument maker's workshop. Later he studied at night classes, finally qualifying as a surgeon in 1893, and worked in the Pathological Department of the Royal Infirmary. He was intensely progressive in outlook, highly outspoken on the prison system of correction, and like Salmon a venomous critic of officialdom.[10] Perhaps through this friendship James became involved with the fledgling Garden City Association and its pre-

1903 caricature explaining the new title of the practice. James is shown in the middle (over the word 'Son') — sporting a broad brimmed hat to make up for his lack of height!

occupation with the problems of urban living for the industrial lower classes (he particularly noted the restrictive effect of contemporary land valuation legislation on building development).[11] The respect held for Salmon in this field was such that he was invited onto the same committee as Mackintosh to assess designs for a 'Cheap Cottage' competition and later designed a proposed Garden City at Cove Farm on the outskirts of Gourock.[12]

His readiness to offer an opinion revealed a headstrong side to his character and he could act impetuously on occasion. One such incident during construction work for Kilmacolm Golf Club (of which he was a committee member) led to a formal reprimand as the appropriate authority from the General Committee had not been given. In spite of such slips Salmon was in demand. As a writer, assessor and tutor, he gave lectures to the architecture students of the Glasgow School of Art, the members of the Glasgow Architectural Association, and the Liberal and Art Clubs.

In terms of design the firm remained active, but in terms of built production the firm's output gradually diminished. Three commissions for office blocks in 1902 all failed to get beyond the

Dr James Devon (b.1866). *The Bailie,* 1909.

British Linen Bank, 110 Queen Street, Glasgow, 1903, photographed by Annan, *c.*1906.

drawing board stage. Apart from the Lion Chambers, 1904-07 (which may have been one of the 1902 schemes at a preliminary stage), and a difficult but individual addition to David Hamilton's British Linen Bank, Queen Street, 1903, large scale commercial commissions all but disappeared. An earlier intriguing Arts and Crafts office design, with steel frame and curtain walls — possibly for the British Linen Bank at Shore Street, Oban — unfortunately was never realised and hinted at what was to come. The British Linen Bank did retain their faith in the firm with James executing work for the Trongate branch in 1903, and travelling as far afield as Thurso, Stromness and Kirkwall on their behalf in 1905; but only small-scale branch adaptations were carried out. Two ecclesiastical schemes for St Peter's, Brown Street, and the Catholic Apostolic Church, McAslin Street, produced fine interior

renovations, but no new design opportunities. The firm received a welcome boost with the commission for a school at Cartsburn in Greenock, 1906-09, and although this project resulted in a new-build scheme, it did not lead to further commissions in the education sector. Domestic work in Kilmacolm, Edzell and Glasgow allowed James to continue to rationalise his design ideas, and also provided steady if somewhat limited income. A development by the firm for co-ownership cottages in Kilmacolm, 1909, demonstrated another side to their own business instincts, and confirmed the simplification occurring in their work. Unfortunately jobs were also lost to others. At the firm's expense Frank Burnet secured tenements at High Street and Duke Street in a limited competition run by the City Improvement Trust — according to young James by 'having back stair influence'. While

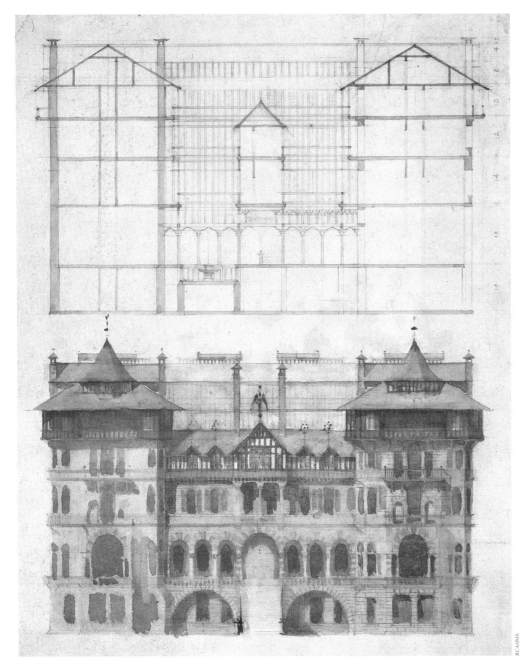

RCAHMS

Municipal Office and Bank,
Shore Street, *c.*1900.
Sketch design, possibly for Oban.

Catholic Apostolic Church, McAslin Street, Glasgow, 1905-06. *The British Architect*, 1906.

Salmon portrays himself dispatching a 'competitor' thereby removing the chance of 'back-stair' influence taking place in architectural competitions! Sketch *c*.1899.

Burnet, Campbell, and Miller continued to gain commissions designing in rational classical idioms, Glasgow Stylists such as Mackintosh, and Salmon and Gillespie, found work more difficult to come by. If the public's loss of interest was expressed through a lack of patronage, the young students at the Art School expressed their opinions less discreetly. They questioned the relevancy of the Glasgow Stylists, and Mackintosh in particular, in savage terms:

'the New Art dines well ... rumour has it that his practice is to assist his digestion by copious draughts of the New Art spirit ... the final horror of New Art is ... Much though they struggle against the great 'checked' monster ... [that] ... Slowly the square-dotted veil drops before their eyes, effectually destroying their vision'.[13]

Having established their name designing in their own distinctive idiom, Salmon and Gillespie pursued work over the next few years and entered competitions with greater frequency. The schemes included the Free Baroque of Rutherglen Library, 1902; the Arts

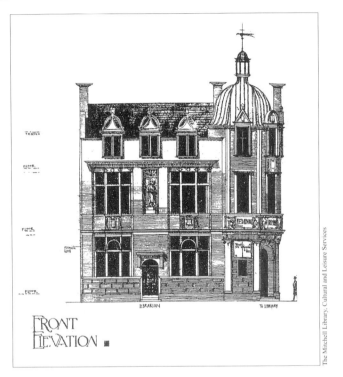

Competition entry for Public Library, Main Street, Rutherglen, 1902. *The British Architect,* 1902.

and Crafts of Newton Park School, Ayr, 1902; the simplified Gothic of Elgin Place Church Mission Halls and Renfrew Parish Halls, both 1903; the Early Renaissance of Hamilton Municipal Buildings, 1903; and the Baroque of Kirkintilloch Municipal Buildings, 1904. The stylistic variation of the entries strongly suggests a search for a theme to meet with contemporary approval. The firm had gained a reputation for aesthetic honesty and integrity in their buildings but it is worth noting that two schemes for the Mitchell Library, Glasgow, 1905, and the Glamorgan County Offices, 1909, had concealed reinforced concrete structures hidden behind elevations that were respectively Renaissance and Free Baroque in style — the presence of the structural systems being suppressed behind historicist façades. Although Salmon had stated that concrete must be treated with respect for its unique properties and Gillespie won a competition for a Ferro-Concrete shop because of the integrity of the design, the contradiction between theory and practice of the Glasgow and

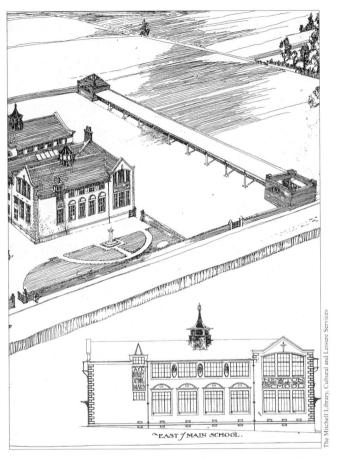

Competition entry for Newton Park School, Ayr, 1902: perspective drawing by John Gaff Gillespie. *The British Architect,* 1902.

Glamorgan schemes may be attributed to the need to conform to styles which would win competitions and bring in finance to the practice. Other competition entries of this period included a design for Perth Town Hall, 1907, in a simple Palladian style; Baroque with *fin-de-siècle* Glasgow nuances for London County Hall, 1907; a very interesting Arts and Crafts inspired Salmon design for a Cottage Hospital in Blantyre, 1908; a Baroque opera-house mode for Hamilton New Academy, 1909; and sixteenth century Scottish for an extension to Rutherglen Town Hall, 1909. While editors and publishers gave them welcome publicity, unfortunately none of these designs resulted in a commission. Success did

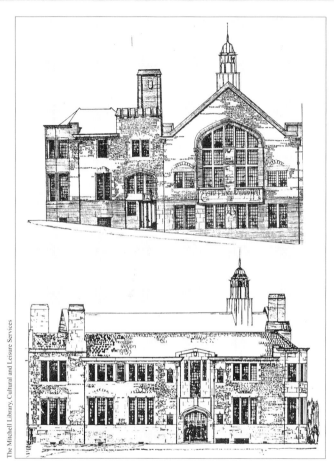

Competition entry for Elgin Place Mission Halls, Dobbies Loan, Glasgow, 1903. *The British Architect,* 1903.

Competition entry for new Municipal Offices, Glamorgan County Council, Glamorgan, 1909. *The British Architect,* 1909.

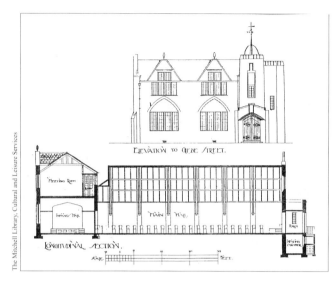

Competition entry for Renfrew Parish Church, Glebe Street, Glasgow, 1903. *The British Architect,* 1903

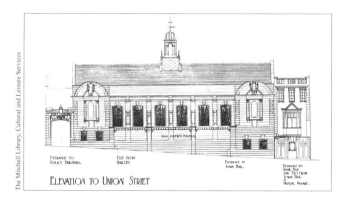

Competition entry for Hamilton Municipal Buildings and Library, Cadzow Street, Hamilton, 1903. *The British Architect,* 1903.

Competition entry for Kirkintilloch Municipal Buildings, Kirkintilloch, 1904.
The British Architect, 1904.

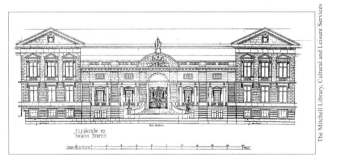

Competition entry for the Mitchell Library, North Street, Glasgow, 1905.
The British Architect, 1905.

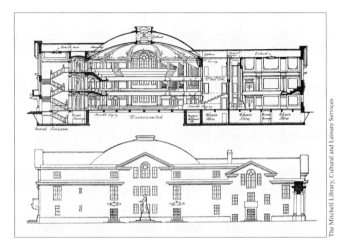

Competition entry for new Town Hall, Perth, 1907. Koch. A., *British Competitions,*
1907.

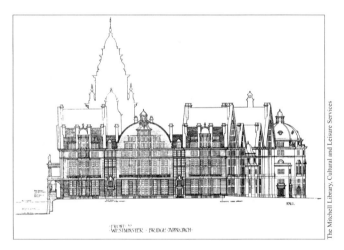

Competition entry for London County Halls, Westminster Bridge-Belvedere Road,
London, 1907. *The British Architect,* 1907.

finally arrive in 1908 when the firm won the prestigious competition for the new Stirling Municipal Buildings with a Baronial inspired scheme designed by Gillespie. Construction, however, was some years away and the practice's resources continued to be stretched. A welcome commission for the Steel Company of Scotland in 1910 produced a simple but well balanced office design in brick with stone dressings which appears to have been executed by Gillespie. But by the end of the decade Salmon and Gillespie had completed the Lion Chambers as their last major joint commission and were designing independently of each other.

The separation had in fact been hinted at in their submission for the new Glasgow and West of Scotland Technical College competition, 1901, which comprised two alternative elevations submitted for the same plans. One was a simple treatment of Italian Renaissance forms by Gillespie and the other an exuberant Glasgow Style scheme using ogee curved pediments, dormers with finials, and sweeping eaves by Salmon.[14] The situation became more apparent in their later individual competition entries: Salmon for the Liberal Club, 1907; and Gillespie for the Stirling Municipal Buildings already mentioned. The relationship would probably have been strained further by Salmon's absences from the office, and his activities outside architecture. He continued to enjoy frequent trips to London and the Continent, wrote and lectured, championed political and social issues — which sometimes risked alienating potential clients — and also found time to pursue the new travel opportunities automobile ownership provided, even publishing a comparative account — with sketches — of a yachting holiday in *Motoring World* in 1910. In a letter to Hugh of 18 August 1910 he hinted, however, that he was short of income. All of these interests out-with the business of architecture would come to a sudden and abrupt end.

Following a short period of illness William Forrest Salmon died of cancer on 7 October 1911. A letter from James to Hugh movingly records their father's last hours and the subsequent journey of the mourners from Kilmacolm to Edinburgh to lay his remains to rest beside their mother, Jessie. It is the only time James refers to his stepmother positively.

In the last years of his life William Forrest changed his will several times, but finally settled on leaving his personal estate jointly to Agnes his widow, and his two sons James and Hugh. A codicil of 1908 established that Rowantreehill could be sold and its value realised but conspicuous by its absence, was any

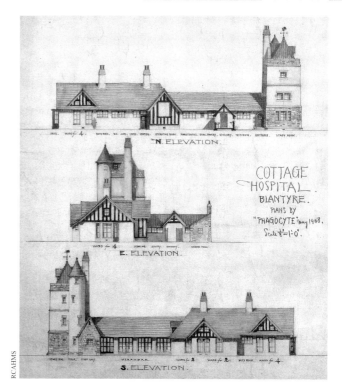

Competition entry for Cottage Hospital, Blantyre, 1908. Submitted by the firm under the pseudonym "Phagocyte."

reference to his share in the business. This omission may have been fatal for the practice as it appears to have left Agnes with a 'sleeping partner' interest that James could not afford to buy out, and Gillespie did not want. Gillespie, now senior-partner, may have forced the final decision. It is suffice to say that within 18 months of William's death James and John agreed to dissolve their partnership. Gillespie appears to have bought out all the others' interests in the business as he remained in the Mercantile Chambers, retaining his successful competition entry for the Stirling Municipal Buildings. Although Salmon retained the projected Garden City development at Gourock, he moved out. He also lost Rowantreehill, the family home he designed.

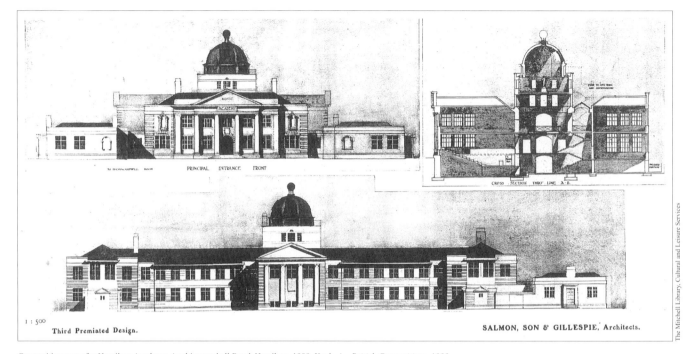

PRINCIPAL ENTRANCE FRONT

CROSS SECTION THRO' LINE A-B.

1 : 500

Third Premiated Design.

SALMON, SON & GILLESPIE, Architects.

Competition entry for Hamilton Academy, Auchincampbell Road, Hamilton, 1909. Koch. A., *British Competitions,* 1909.

Competition entry for the Glasgow & West of Scotland Technical College, George Street, Glasgow, 1901. The simplified Renaissance perspective drawing is by Gillespie, and the Glasgow Style elevation by Salmon. *The British Architect,* 1901.

'A man willing to work, and unable to find work, is perhaps the saddest sight that fortune's inequality exhibits under the sun.'

Thomas Carlyle, *Chartism* (1839)

BIOGRAPHY: 1913-1924: FINAL YEARS

By the end of 1913 Glasgow's economy was struggling. Although the city had increased its boundaries in 1912 and was seen as more 'responsible than any other city or town in the United Kingdom for the spread … of municipal progress',[1] the major industries of cotton, glass, pottery, and iron production, upon which much of Glasgow's wealth had been built, were waning. Shipping and shipbuilding continued to flourish but the threat of war and the associated arms race did not encourage investors. The Dean of Guild records show that applications for private housing works dropped from over 4,000 in 1902, to around 250 by 1911 as

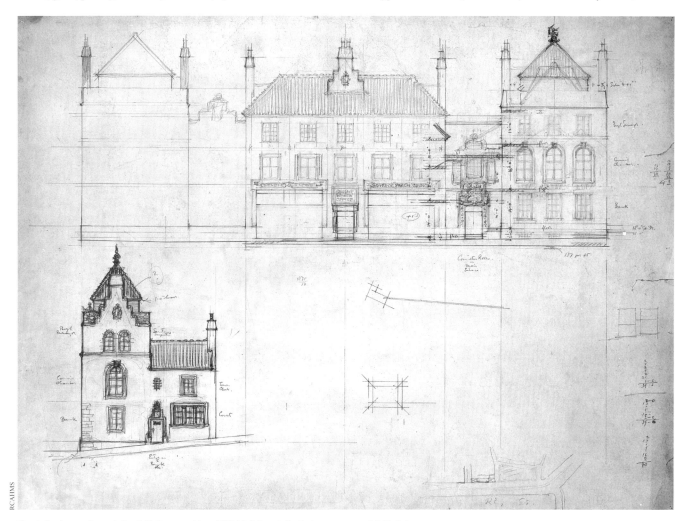

Sketch for the new Gourock Burgh Halls competition, 1914-15. Salmon's final scheme was awarded third place.

developers responded to Lloyd George's 'People's Budget' of 1909-10, which put a 20% tax on the increment value of all heritable property, and which was described as 'the final stroke against all speculative building'.[2] The city turned its back on its most gifted designers, losing much of its interest in the decorative arts, and the practitioners of the Glasgow Style, who had been lauded and supported both in Glasgow and on the Continent, found themselves outcast. C. R. Mackintosh and his wife Margaret Macdonald found the atmosphere in the city so inimical that on a moment's decision they left to join the Newberys at Walberswick in 1914,[3] leaving the MacNairs, Herbert and Frances, in Glasgow. Only Jessie King and her husband E. A. Taylor, who had left the city in 1906 to work in Manchester, continued to enjoy a degree of popular acclaim for their designs, but even they never returned to work in Glasgow and instead set up a studio in Paris in 1911. The Taylors continued to correspond with their friends in Glasgow including Salmon[4] who, following the dissolution of the partnership and the sale of the family home, moved to the city to live and begin practice on his own from a flat at 48 Jane Street, Blythswood Square.

Although work at this time does not appear to have been abundant he remained active. His medical contacts resulted in commissions for a garage for Dr J. Green at 1-3 Richmond Street, Glasgow, 1914, and interior alterations for Dr J. T. West at

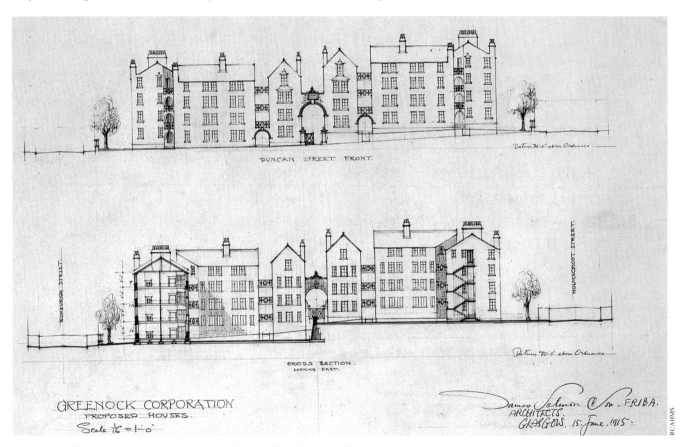

A design and build competition entry for a housing scheme at Roxburgh Street, Greenock, 1915.

Hostel at Flotta, 1917 (sketch drawn from a photograph in the Annual Report of the SNC of the YMCA).

'Hastings Lodge', St Andrews Drive the following year. Also in 1915 he entered a very personal Baronial design for the Gourock Burgh Halls competition which won third prize. He followed this with a housing scheme for the Greenock Corporation at Roxburgh Street, and a series of small cottages for Samuel Galley at Eastfield in Cambuslang.[5] While these projects confirmed his interest in the design of housing for lower income groups neither, unfortunately, seems to have been built. Early in 1916 the Admiralty decided to proceed with his Garden City proposals at Cove Farm near Gourock, which provided accommodation for workers engaged in armaments manufacture. However the local council was unable to offer the support it had previously promised, which doubtless led to the development extending over only four to five acres rather than the 38 originally planned. Sadly no details of the scheme or its architectural quality are known at this time. James's association with the Admiralty continued through the war years and resulted in a steady stream of commissions for huts, hostels and canteens.[6] It also provided income when fee-earning opportunities were limited. Despite the war and his own difficult situation he was never idle and apart from competitions he involved himself in schemes and ideas for many subjects. He took it upon himself to redesign the cars used in Glasgow's tramway system, producing a 'car de luxe'.[7] He even devised a system of counting based on an eight-digit limit of numbers. He advocated this 'Octal System', which was similar to the binary system taught today but with an octanumerous scale, as a means of measuring areas and weights, and time and money; for which he designed clock and coinage systems.[8] He remained opinionated, having no qualms about saying precisely what he thought and readily acknowledging himself to be 'a social and municipal Bolshevic'.[9] While his views on the Parish Council, School Board and Infirmary Managers were considered unprintable, it was reported that he thought the Glasgow Corporation officials' efforts 'to destroy our finest buildings is due to the hope that in time their own will be the best left — but he thinks this would entail too much destruction!'[10] He believed that architects had to concern themselves with all matters influencing the creation of architecture, including legislation. He lobbied MPs generally and the Chancellor of the Exchequer, David Lloyd George, specifically, for action to be taken to relieve the limitations of the 1909-10 Budget (noted earlier) which taxed 'every shilling's worth of building ... [while] land kept out of use [was] relieved of taxation. Could any two incarnations of the Devil … do more harm to building'?[11] Salmon's concern was not only for the economic damage of the legislation to the business of architecture, but that it would ultimately have a detrimental affect on the quality and standard of the building fabric. He argued that 'We are suffering from — not a mere window tax — but a floor, wall and roof tax, a fireplace tax, a bathroom tax, a tax on health — on life itself'.[12] For Salmon, people, their living conditions, and quality of life were all bound up and dependent on good architecture and the tax was a moral injustice.[13]

His altruistic concerns were reinforced by his marriage on St Valentine's Day, 14 February 1917 to Dr Agnes Picken, a colleague of Dr Devon's at Duke Street Prison.[14] She was a well-regarded practitioner in what was then a male dominated environment. Resolute and no nonsense, she had made her own way in the world of medicine, and was remembered by the family as being both very direct and amusing. One of her friends, Dr Katherine McPhail, had left Glasgow for Belgrade — capital of the newly formed state of Jugoslavia — to work in a hospital caring for refugee children who had been abandoned and displaced at the end of the recent hostilities. Dr McPhail corresponded with Dr Picken about her work and encouraged her to visit the hospital, possibly also asking for her assistance. When the Salmons learned of the poor health and living conditions of the orphans, they resolved to help in any way they could.

Directly following the war Salmon's architectural output appears to have almost ceased. He had prepared sketch designs for two theatres in Glasgow: one titled 'The Lantern' in Bothwell Street,

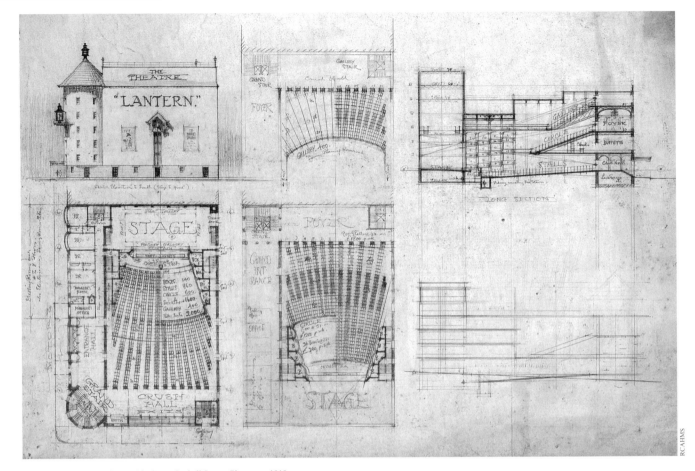

Sketch for the Lantern Theatre, Pitt Street-Bothell Street, Glasgow, *c.*1919.

the other in Richard Street. Although he carried out meticulous studies of existing theatres and prepared budget cost information for his schemes, neither was pursued beyond the sketch stage. A later competition submission for a war memorial in Campbeltown resulted in an ornate Celtic-inspired design which comprised a stone cairn raised on a mound, itself crowned with a galley in bronze and bordered by a great circle of standing stones. Salmon directed that the men of Campbeltown would each bring a stone for the dyke, and each women a basket of earth to form the mound. The standing stones were to be brought by the regiments

of the fallen. The cairn itself would contain relics secured behind bronze doors bearing the names of those lost. Salmon wanted to create a memorial that formed a communion between the living community and those lost from it in the war. Sadly this poetic and poignant scheme was not selected by the assessors.

A holiday to Norway during July and August of 1920 gave the Salmons a chance to rest and relax. They sailed firstly to Stavanger, thereafter travelling to Odde and Bergen by a combination of steamship and train. Salmon was very taken by the spectacular landscape and enjoyed being close to nature. Journeys

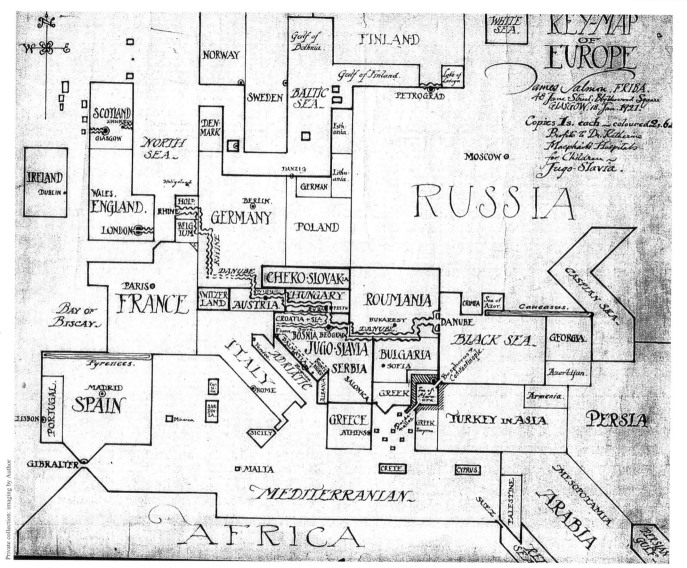

Salmon's cubist-style *Map of Europe*, prepared to raise funds for Dr McPhail's Hospitals for Children in Belgrade, 1921. He explored 'Cubism' in other sketches.

amongst the fjords and glaciers were followed by treks in the hills. On one walk lasting two hours he and Agnes climbed over 3,300ft above sea level. They also visited many little villages, Salmon taking time-out to study the carving details of local churches.

Returning to Glasgow recharged, they decided to take up Dr McPhail's earlier invitation and set off for Serbia on 3rd October. Travelling from London on the Simplon Orient Express, they visited both Paris and Venice *en route* to Belgrade. They were so

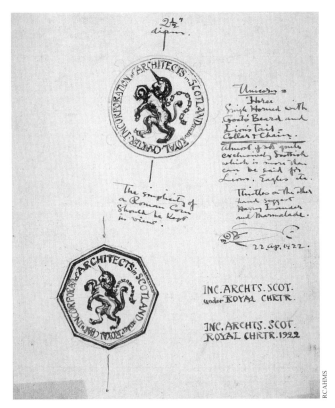

A sketch prepared for the emblem of the new Incorporation of Architects in Scotland, 1922 — the octagonal geometry of the background was changed to pentagonal in the published version.

Sir Christopher Wren, sketch prepared for *The Quarterly*, 1923.

moved by Dr McPhail's young charges that Dr Picken decided to stay on and directly assist while Salmon returned home to start fundraising work.

For a time the hospital rented a house for use as a sanatorium from the government, the 'Villa Bravaçic' in Dubrovnik. However, when the authorities decided to sell the property, the hospital was faced with the ultimatum of either purchasing the building or moving out.[15] The villa was located on the outskirts of the town overlooking the Adriatic coast of Croatia, and Salmon, who visited it on a number of occasions, considered its idyllic location and facilities perfect for the recovery and well being of the children. He was so determined to help raise the necessary finance to purchase the property he involved himself heavily in the setting up

of a fund raising committee, and wrote articles for the local and national press about the hospital and its work to encourage donations.

He produced a remarkable illustrated map of Europe in a geometrical-cubist style, of which copies were made for sale — 1*s.* uncoloured, and 2*s.* 6*d.* coloured. He also gave addresses to clubs and societies, including the Liberal Club and the Glasgow Art Club to stir up awareness and support. The latter held a dinner to allow him to specifically appeal on behalf of the hospital,[16]

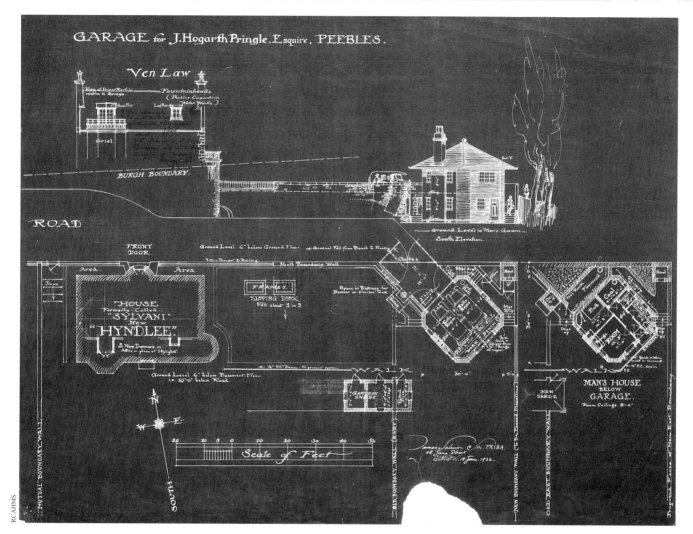

GARAGE for J. Hogarth Pringle, Esquire, PEEBLES.

'Hyndlee,' Venlaw Road, Peebles, 1922. The two levels of the chauffeur's house merge into the landscape, the wide overhanging roof enclosing both building and surrounding topography.

during which he entertained the company with travelogue anecdotes. One journey from Belgrade to Sarajevo stuttered to disaster when his party's transport broke down, and they had to be put up in a church. Salmon recalled that before going to sleep on the floor he had one last smoke to relax and unwittingly used a holy vessel as an ashtray!

A humanitarian, Salmon willingly gave his time freely to many worthy causes, particularly those promoting charitable aid and those fostering architecture and the arts. Besides the Liberal Club and the Glasgow Art Club, he was a member of the Chelsea Art Club, the Scottish Society of Art Workers, the Scottish Guild of Handicraft, the Glasgow Hammermen, the Wrights, the West of

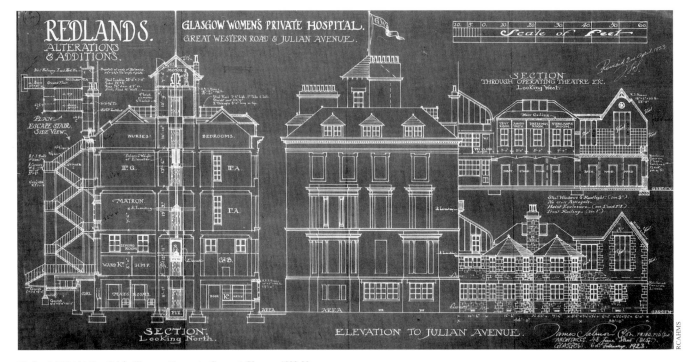

'Redlands,' District Hospital for Women at Lancaster Crescent, Glasgow, 1922-23.

Scotland Garden City Association, and the Glasgow Institute of Architects. A council member of the GIA from 1918, he became one of four vice-presidents serving on the committees for working class housing competitions, for town planning, for practice, and for the Institute's library and education. A founder member of the Institute of Scottish Architects from its creation in 1916, he became a representative for the Glasgow chapter when the Institute became the Incorporation of Architects in Scotland under Royal Charter on 6 May 1922. Again he became an office bearer, sitting on the committees responsible for housing and town planning, for competitions, and for establishing the architects' scale of fees. He was also the convenor and first editor for the bulletin of the Incorporation known as *The Quarterly*, contributing articles, sketches and photographs from his own travels. In the course of his duties he presented proposals on conditions for competitions to the Royal Institute of British Architects in London in 1922, which were reported to have been favourably received.[17] He was instrumental in attracting an exhibition of American

Architecture to the McLellan Galleries in Glasgow, which opened on 23 June 1922. This touring collection of drawings and photographs came via Paris and London and included work by such masters as Burnham, Hunt, Post, Richards, Sullivan and Goodhue. Salmon rated Louis Sullivan's National Farmer's Bank, Owatonna, Minnesota — with its large arch forms penetrating a very basic geometrical cube set off with decorative highlights — as the most original design on show. But not all the American masters were so warmly received. He noted that 'One gets tired of guessing which old building Messrs McKim Mead & White will copy next. Their office must have a photograph of every box-office success in Europe'![18] Salmon attributed this 'failing' to the education of the American architect. 'Her [America's] architects are products of the hot-house schools of Paris, trained in rigid styles by the French architect dominie. Architecture has never been understood by the French. They look on it as cabinetmaking in stone. The Americans suffer from having gone to school there instead of playing truant'![19] Perhaps this comment also pokes gentle fun at those Scots-born architects who were also Paris-trained, such as the formidable Burnet and Keppie, whom Salmon knew and drew comic caricatures of while attending Glasgow Art Club dinners with his artist friends!

In the autumn of 1922 Salmon submitted a design in an outrageous Scots Baronial style for the open international competition for the new offices of the *Chicago Tribune* newspaper. The design was in two distinct parts. The lower section comprised a tall simple block of canted bay forms, while the upper section was in complete contrast, taking the style of a Baronial castle with castellated walls and corner turrets. The total composition appeared like a scenic picture of a Scottish stronghold atop a rocky outcrop somewhere in the Highlands. Only the piper was missing! The competition drew many frivolous entries, among them the monumental Doric column scheme of Adolf Loos and the gigantic 'Indian Chief' design of Mossdorf, Hahn and Busch.[20] Bearing in mind Salmon's sense of humour and the existence of a comical sketch of a 'Scotch Baronial' castle he jotted down on the back of a circular from this period, it is difficult to imagine his entry as anything more than a flight of fancy. Salmon also knew that even if he won he would never see his scheme built — he had been diagnosed as suffering from cancer and could not expect to live for more than a few years longer. Despite his health problems he continued working 'and faced the situation with his usual courage'.[21]

In the same year as the Tribune Tower competition he produced two designs for houses. The first for Mr W. K. Rodger — a solicitor from Rutherglen — appears not to have been developed beyond the sketch design stage, but the second for Mrs Hogarth Pringle at Hyndlee, Venlaw Road, Peebles was built. The major part of this work comprised the design of a two storey chauffeur's house with an integral garage.[22] The plan took the basic form of a square with the corners truncated to form an unequal sided octagon, the geometrical aspect further emphasised by a simple over-sailing pyramidal roof. It was very cleverly planned and orientated to take account of extremely difficult site levels. The garage was located at the high ground road entrance level, with the accommodation placed underneath at the lower garden level. A small stepped path, cut-in between the outside walls and the adjacent banking, not only provided access between the two tiers, but also formed a link between building and land. The house itself was placed into the raking landscape at an angle and recalled the work of Frank Lloyd Wright in its relationship with the topography.

Towards the end of 1922 he was appointed to convert and extend Redlands, a large Italianate villa of 1869, into Redlands Hospital for Women, Lancaster Crescent, Great Western Road, Glasgow. The design opportunities were somewhat limited but he invested individuality by adopting a pair of part-detached octagonal forms for the extension and incorporating an extensive area of patent glazing — juxtaposing the total against the conservatism of the original building. He also designed furnishings and individual sanitary fittings, including a combined wash basin and bath.

Throughout 1923 Salmon's health deteriorated. A sailing holiday on the Norfolk Broads provided a chance to sketch and rest afloat, but as he could no longer walk more than a hundred yards his opportunities to visit nearby historical buildings, as he had done in the past, were restricted. Despite his poor physical condition his mind remained sharp and critical. Recounting details from his recent holiday in *The Quarterly*, he took the opportunity to question the religious morals of the clergymen of Ely Cathedral. He also observed more generally that, 'the attitude of the present vicars, rectors, and such like ... have little in common with the builders of the old churches which they use. In a way they suggest hermit crabs who, having no proper skins of their own, wriggle into the deserted abodes of defunct shellfish'.[23] His imminent passing clearly did not alter his views of clerics and traditional religious faiths. There was no rediscovery or rebirth of the Christian beliefs of his father and grandfather, and no departing from his agnosticism.

To add to the sense of times passing his Aunt Mina, to whom he had remained close, became ill with arteriosclerosis and was taken into Craighouse private mental hospital in Edinburgh. She died on 9 January 1924 and it fell to James, despite his own poor health, to conclude her personal affairs.

As winter progressed towards spring his strength ebbed away. Although Dr Devon had moved to Saughton Prison, Edinburgh, he wrote regular letters to Salmon recounting news, anecdotes, and meetings with mutual acquaintances, in an effort to try and lift the spirits of his ailing friend.[24]

But despite these words of support Salmon, one of Glasgow's most important designers, died at his home in Jane Street at 11.40am on 27 April 1924. He had just turned 51.

His death marked the end of an architectural dynasty stretching back almost 100 years, but surprisingly his passing was not especially remarked upon. There was a somewhat standardised obituary in *The RIBA Journal* and a general notice in *The*

HORNING QUAY. 1923.

Horning Quay, Norfolk Broads, 1923, later published in *The Quarterly*.

Quarterly — but none of his fellow professionals were moved to write any words of remembrance, nor a commentary on his architecture in any form. When John Gaff Gillespie died two years later in 1926, and Mackintosh in 1928, they fared little better. This was perhaps a reflection of the general view held of the Glasgow Stylists at the time. For all the significance of their work during a 20 year period — in which they had demonstrated how Art Nouveau, and then subsequently Modernism, offered radical solutions to the dilemmas of contemporary British architecture — when they passed away, they were practically ignored. Certainly their best work was behind them, but more through a lack of opportunity than any lack of talent. Their reputations had been eclipsed by Burnet, Rowand Anderson, Washington Browne, Miller, and others who, although talented designers in their own ways, had achieved greater commercial success by continuing to explore traditional building styles. Salmon referred back to historical movements only to learn from them, neither to copy nor develop their languages. Like Mackintosh, he was inspired by an entirely different inner-spirit than that motivating the Beaux Art trained Burnet and others. Salmon and Mackintosh were impelled to explore the aesthetic possibilities one could encounter stepping outwith the confines of convention. But as was his nature Salmon 'leaped' even further than his Glasgow Style friend. He whole-heartedly embraced the new technologies and materials available to him, and exploited the fresh expressive possibilities they offered. In this respect he was in every sense a true Modernist.

Private Collection: Photograph by Author

The artist Denovan Adam junior.

'All things return eternally, and ourselves with them:
we have already existed times without number,
and all things with us.'

Friedrich Wilhelm Nietzsche, *Thus Spake Zarathustra* (1883-92)

'Time present and time past are both perhaps present in time
future, and time future contained in time past.'

T. S. Eliot, *Burnt Norton*

PHILOSOPHY

James Salmon's writings reveal him to be an independent personality who revelled in the discussion and pursuit of architecture, the arts, and politics. They also reveal him to be a humorous, strong-willed, and serious individual with a distinctive view of man and his meaning on this earth. In 1909 he published a two-part article entitled 'The Art of Building' in which he revealed his innermost thoughts and beliefs, his architecture being a direct reflection of this philosophy.

Salmon believed conscious life to be 'one united thing throughout infinity and eternity'[1] and that the soul of man, or collective unconscious, could not be destroyed any more 'than either matter or physical energy'.[2] While man the individual occupied only a fleeting moment in a continuum of time and space, the society to which man belonged included the whole cosmos as well as the human race. Through knowledge Salmon believed that each soul could stretch back into whatever place and time its consciousness took it, and hence stretch its roots back across the centuries and entwine 'among the civilisations thousands of years old'.[3] At the end of our time on earth 'we, as individuals, melt into a larger unity from which again life flows into all living things',[4] and we are in our present manifestation 'but the expression of a piece of divine essence ... [through which] ... We are united to space and eternity, in which all consciousness is one'.[5] This unity or divine essence from which the soul derived, Salmon likened to the concept of *Beauty* of the ancient Greeks. It applied to the whole order of the Universe and formed the source from which all things derived and to which all things returned to rise again. This philosophy is in some respects similar to the pantheistic religion of the ancient Celtic tribes. Echoing Salmon's all-infusing *Beauty*, they believed that rivers, trees, mountains and stones were all objects of veneration encompassing the implicit and immanent spiritual vitality of nature. Salmon also utilised this concept linking the symbolism of trees of Eternal Life and Knowledge to his concept of *Beauty*. Mackintosh had earlier explored this theme in his watercolours *The Tree of Personal Effort* and *The Tree of Influence*. It was a rhythm and melody of life which 'pervaded the land, the sea, the heavens and the people',[6] indeed all physical objects and metaphysical ideals. To study this *Beauty* 'was to understand and enter into the eternal life of the divinities — to find, grasp and comprehend the meaning of this painted show in which we are the puppets'.[7] For Salmon, man was the conduit for the manifestation of this *Beauty* and architecture

Courtesy of Mrs Anne Francis

James Salmon outside Rowantreehill, 1904.

was the principal art through which this spirit could be expressed, because 'lying inter-woven with every building is the nature of men ... [and that] ... the art of it, that is its inherent significance'[8] was 'the expression of the Eternal God within the passing man'.[9]

Salmon wrote that in architecture 'No phrase wrings fuller with falsity than "*the use transcends the beauty*" ... What in the name of all the gods, can be more useful than beauty? What, in the name of all the goddesses, can be of any use whatever, if it is not beautiful? "Beauty" and "use" are one, and everything else is "useless" and "ugly"'.[10] Salmon extended this equalization of beauty and use to that of architecture and building and in turn brought himself into direct conflict with John Ruskin. Salmon said 'Ruskin is fundamentally wrong when he says that architecture must be carefully distinguished from building. Building is Architecture. If we could found a school of architecture which stuck to the sane building of buildings, getting down to the bedrock of absolute economy, we would exercise a good and powerful influence on methods of building throughout the world, and gradually reduce the pet creations of the flash builder and flash architect to objects of pity or perhaps amusement'.[11]

The architectural views of Salmon and Ruskin are distinguished by their differing beliefs and definition of the word 'use'. Ruskin, a fervent Christian, wrote that whatever enables man to fulfil his use and function 'to be the witness of the Glory of God ... is, in the pure and first sense of the word Useful ... But things that only help us to exist are, (*only*) in a secondary and mean sense, useful',[12] and 'remember that the most beautiful things in the world are the most useless'.[13]

Salmon, an agnostic, did not share Ruskin's religious precepts or his dismissal of the beauty of function. Mackintosh, when addressing the Glasgow Architectural Association in 1892, quoted George Gilbert Scott as saying, 'if we look around throughout the creations of nature we are prompted to reply that in linking beauty with utility we are more directly imitating 'him' ... in whose works the union of the useful and beautiful is one of the most universal characteristics'.[14] Other critics such as Geoffrey Scott also challenged Ruskin's application of religious morality to architecture, most particularly in his discussion of 'The Ethical Fallacy' in *The Architecture of Humanism*.

Like Ruskin, however, Salmon did recognise the difference between building and architecture, noting that 'Architecture if it can be distinguished from building is the part which appeals to the soul as the other part serves the body',[15] but he also considered them interdependent as opposed to mutually exclusive and equated them in parallel with beauty and use. He clarified this relationship further when considering the bond between science and art, writing 'Science is the study of the material world. Every new discovery enables us to give a new form of expression to ourselves',[16] and 'Without science, art is powerless'.[17] In architecture, because of the direct inter-relationships existing between science and art which constantly vary with time and economic change, the art in a building would always reflect that period or moment in the continuum of time when it was conceived and realised.

Accordingly if an architect utilised contemporary scientific discoveries and physical resources in an ordered, reasoned and economic manner, he would naturally express himself in a fitting way without having to concern himself with being 'new' or 'modern'. He wrote:

'Science is the gathering together of the material
Art is the thing expressed by its rearrangement.
Science makes the sound.
Art is the sense.
Science moulds the form.
Art is its meaning.
Science is the action.
Art is its significance.
Oh! Sound without sense,
Form without meaning,
Action without significance
How wearisome you are'! [18]

Salmon advocated the study of ancient buildings to learn the science of building and to understand their meanings, but he vehemently abhorred the notion of copying the ancient styles for their own sake. To copy is 'to rewrite a tale that is already written',[19] and to design in ignorance of the meanings of mouldings and ornament in architecture is comparable to 'the mouthings of prayers by sanctimonious hypocrites, by jabbering idiots and religious maniacs'.[20] His designs accordingly evolved from a recognition and appreciation of the advantages both economical and physical of modern materials and methods of construction, combined with a knowledge and understanding of historical formal languages of architecture. In summation, Salmon viewed life and existence as an infinite flux of generation, degeneration and regeneration and architecture as *the* tangible reflection of this state.

Salmon's views were not unique. As early as 1884, while addressing the Sunday Society in Glasgow, Oscar Wilde claimed that 'all the beautiful things had been made when something useful was attempted, and all ugly things when something beautiful was tried'.[21] The English architect W. R. Lethaby (1857-1931) referred to architecture as one of 'the endeavours of men to link through their craft with the Universe',[22] and argued that fulfilling human needs in an orderly and scientific way would produce good building thereby tying architecture to the process of living and solving problems. Like Salmon, the German architect and critic Gottfried Semper had earlier rejected attempts at sham styling. Semper additionally argued that the study of historical style involved not only the academic examination of proportion, details and fabric, but also the study of the past lives of our ancestors. He wrote 'The ... characteristics of the different systems of architecture will remain obscure to us, as long as we have no idea of the social, political and religious combinations of those nations and ages to which these styles of architecture belonged'.[23] Mackintosh's view that 'all great and living architecture has been the direct expression, of the needs & beliefs of man at the time of its creation',[24] also very closely reflects Salmon's recognition of the importance of the period and spirit of the age to architecture. The artist Wassily Kandinsky (1866-1924) also noted the uniqueness of each period of artistic expression, declaring that 'Every work of art is the child of its age and ... each period of culture produces an art of its own which can never be repeated. Efforts to re-live the art-principles of the past will at best produce an art that is still-born'.[25] Mackintosh also referred to the transient nature of architecture, observing that 'Behind every style of architecture is an earlier style in which the germ of every form is to be found ... all is the slow change of growth ... [and] ... in the far larger sence [sic] all architecture is one, when traced back through the streams of civilisations as they followed or influenced one another'.[26] While Mackintosh borrowed here from Lethaby's *Architecture, Mysticism and Myth*, recent work by Timothy Neat has also linked the work of 'The Four' to the philosophy of Rosicrucianism and groups such as 'The Golden Dawn'. Across the Atlantic in contemporary Chicago, Louis Sullivan's description of 'The Infinite',[27] that unknown, unseen, unfelt, unheard and untasted energy source which motivates all activity, also bears a remarkable similarity to Salmon's 'unity'.[28] Sullivan also spoke of a religion of architecture and the merging of all knowledge to realise a democratic architecture, i.e. an all-embracing one.

While it is apparent that Salmon's architectural philosophy was not totally unique, his originality lies in his translation of this philosophy in tectonic form.

'Fine art is that in which the hand, the head, and the heart of man go together.'

John Ruskin, *The Two Paths*

'That is Beautiful which is produced by the inner need, which springs from the soul.'

Wassily Kandinsky, *Concerning the Spiritual in Art* (1914)

ARCHITECTURAL ANALYSIS:
THE EARLY WORKS: OF ARCHITECTURE AND SCULPTURE

Salmon's movement away from contemporary forms was first hinted at in a minor addition to Dennistoun Infant School, Roslea Drive, Glasgow, 1895. Involving the erection of a small gymnasium and technical block, it was a plain rectangular grey sandstone building with a slated roof. It was relieved only by isolated carved panels and elongated curved roll mouldings around the entrance doors, perhaps borrowed from Mackintosh's window mouldings at the contemporary Martyrs' Public School, Townhead, Glasgow, or Leiper's earlier Sun Life Insurance Offices.[1] Internally an economy of detailing predominated with only the ends of the tie members to the exposed timber beams being decorated.

Salmon next became involved with new bank premises for the British Linen Company at 215 High Street, Glasgow, 1894-96, located on the original site of the house of Thomas Campbell, the 'poet of freedom'. The design appears to have been by Forrest Salmon in collaboration with John Gaff Gillespie, with James participating in the site and interior works. Planned with offices on the ground floor and two storeys of flats above, it is constructed of Dumfriesshire red sandstone set on a granite base. Asymmetrical in composition, the east elevation has a single large arched window at ground floor level and a stepped gable with crowning figure, all juxtaposed against a corner tower capped with a decorative open campanile above the entrance. Over the main door there is a coloured glass oriel depicting a ship framed in stone — a favorite motif of Stephen Adam junior. A new feature appeared on top of the gable of the north elevation: an ogee-shaped open stone crown, the first occurrence of this element on one of the firm's buildings.[2] Internally there was much interesting detail, notably in the design of the rear office fireplace, which had columns with capitals incorporating cherubs and elongated vertical scrolls.

Prior to these projects Gillespie had completed his first major work with William Forrest Salmon, the design of new offices for the Scottish Temperance League at 116 Hope Street, Glasgow, 1893. The Hope Street elevation is a very lively affair combining arches, scrolls, carving and sculpture in a free interpretation drawn from Antwerp Town Hall. It comprises three main sections. The ground and first floor section is composed of a central double arched ground floor window with a bay window above flanked by two relief figures in medallions. The second and third floor section

The British Linen Bank, 215 High Street, Glasgow, built 1894-96.

The Scottish Temperance League, 116 Hope Street, Glasgow, 1893: perspective drawing by John Gaff Gillespie. *Academy Architecture*, 1894.

The Scottish Temperance League viewed from the south west showing the bay windows repeated by Mackintosh in the adjacent Daily Record Offices, 1900-01.

repeats the double arched window theme of the ground and first and employs individual elongated Corinthian columns to tie the composition together. The third section [fourth floor] has a centrally located single arch window used in combination with curvaceous scrolls, open arches and figures crowning a stepped gable. Although the composition as a whole is generally symmetrical, the canted bay windows which are such a feature of the southern flank elevation are not repeated in the northern.[3] The fine sculpture features were carried out by the prize-winning artist Richard Ferris, a native of the city who had trained at the Glasgow School of Art with Gillespie.[4]

Ferris's services were retained and supplemented by the cosmopolitan English sculptor Francis Derwent Wood (1871-1926) for the firm's next major commercial development, the Mercantile Chambers, 53 Bothwell Street, Glasgow, 1896-98. The building was developed by the Mercantile Chambers Company of which William Forrest Salmon was a shareholder, and provided young James with his first major project. Seven storeys high with a street front elevation over 100 yards long, it was one of the largest steel-framed office blocks in the city and provided a vast area of lettable space, comparable in scale to contemporary developments in Chicago. It required three light-wells within its depth to allow adequate daylighting for offices in the centre of the plan and had two passenger lifts running side by side, the first building in Glasgow to have such an arrangement. The overall pattern of the façade recalls the earlier Scottish Temperance League offices, being composed of gabled end bays, elongated columns and integral relief stone carving, but their proportions are quite different. The Scottish Temperance League is tall and narrow while the Mercantile Chambers is tall and wide. New features such as the column arrangement to the window jambs running through the height of the building at the two end bays, the chequered stone mouldings around the windows, and the depressed ground floor arches have no previous office precedent. Their source can be traced to Leiper and Anderson(?) at the Sun Life Building and Templeton's Carpet Factory. At a detail level James's design departed even further from historicism than these earlier works. The combination of sinuous pilasters, twisted columns, elongation and accentuation of pilaster capitals to integrate with the lintels, and softly rounded treatment of the arch-springing to the ground and upper floor arcades are all quite unique. The columns at high level to the flanking bay windows are very boldly handled, the upper groups having unusual curved eyelets towards their base sections. The gables themselves are finished with carved ogee caps with pinnacles, which are formally mirrored in metalwork in the roof capping of the elongated central dormer. The 'soft' handling of the sinuous 'initial' stone and relief sculptured salmon — acknowledging the authorship of the design — apparently leaping out from within the body of the façade, bear a close affinity with Mackintosh's motif work on the earlier *Glasgow Herald* Offices, Mitchell Street, 1893, and with contemporary sculptural techniques being used on the Continent. For all the originality of the sculpture, *The Builder* noted its spartan distribution, observing that the building 'is excessively plain, and its few scattered

The Mitchell Library, Cultural and Leisure Services

Mercantile Chambers, 53 Bothwell Street, Glasgow, 1896-98: perspective drawing by James Salmon. *Glasgow Advertiser and Property Circular,* 1898.

Front entrance and arch-springing detail, Mercantile Chambers.

Arch motif detail, Glasgow Herald Offices, Mitchell Street, Glasgow, 1893 by C. R. Mackintosh.

Wrought fish detail, Mercantile Chambers.

Canted bay windows to rear of Mercantile Chambers.

ornaments seem merely to accentuate its severe simplicity'.[5] The reviewer continued in less positive fashion, noting 'the composition as a whole has the merit of daring originality ... but ... looks more like the design of a clever academy student'![6] Leiper was more generous, commending it as 'very original and fresh in detail'.[7]

If the front elevation was daring and original, then the rear elevation was even more so. Composed of a grid of bay windows built of steel vertical sections, with lead spandrels between very slim red brick piers, the construction was extremely functional and economic, and the pioneering example of its kind in Glasgow. The only decorative feature on the rear elevation is a single stone block illustrating an elongated tree motif and the name of the building. The forms and detailing of the internal features in the Mercantile Chambers are also very different from those remaining at the Temperance League offices. Reminiscent of the style of the Arts

Glasgow Style watercolour of a house design, dated 'February 1896', possibly for the family home in Kilmacolm.

'Rowantreehill', Rowantreehill Road, Kilmacolm, built 1898.

and Crafts designers in England, the fireplaces have elongated timber columns and pilasters with wide overhanging mantels, and are faced with ceramic tiles with brass hearths similar to the work of C. H. B. Quennell. The door sets have pilasters and lintels identical in overall form to those of the windows, and thus establish a visual link between exterior and interior to achieve a unified composition. Fine stained-glass panels are located in the lightwells at the lower levels, featuring serpents entwining a staff, and sailing ships with billowing sails.

Despite a certain incongruity in the overall compositional balance, the combination and variety of elements create a youthful spirited quality perhaps epitomised in the central angled ogee dormer with its elongated quatrefoil leaded windows. The language begins with Leiper but the spirit is Salmonesque. Jessie Newbery (1864-1948), Francis Newbery's wife, felt that the substantial depths of the cornices, string-courses, and bays, were such that the lights probably had to be put on earlier than in any other office in the city![8]

With the firm's fortunes improving and work increasing, Forrest Salmon moved the family out of the city to a new house in the village of Kilmacolm — west of Glasgow — for which James appears to have prepared a preliminary study in 1896. His watercolour presents a very interesting Arts and Crafts inspired design, combining an oversailingroof and ashlar walling with ogee bay forms and cut-away-corner details. The aesthetic of the illustration itself is also distinctive, the muted colouring and treatment of the trees and plant forms giving a distinctive Glasgow Style flavour. James developed the composition to a much livelier conclusion in 1898, combining a variety of materials, textures and colours with very personalised detailing. Rowantreehill, as it is still known, is sited on a high rocky slope looking west across the Gryffe valley and designed in an English Tudor style similar to Leiper's house designs in Helensburgh. It has snecked rubble walls at ground level and half-timbered walls at the upper floor levels, all capped with a wide overhanging red tiled roof. The robust rafters are stained black, exposed at the eaves, and have arches cut out which evoke the form of open-mouthed fish. Elongated gargoyles to the eaves rafters of the gables, serve not only to decorate but also to emphasise the construction of the house. The windows are all shapes and sizes, square, rectangular, and arched, as well as ogee with a scroll centering like two elongated 'S' shapes. This last type is also mirrored in the boundary walling. The entrance doorway is framed by a sweeping Art Nouveau-inspired stone moulding with an ogee pyramid lamp overhead, held from the wall by flowing tendril-like supports.

This unique personal detailing continues in the internal carved work. Within the entrance lobby there is a fantasy elf figure visiting a rowan tree on a hill; there are golf caricatures in the hall; the seven ages of man, and the earth and the stars in the lounge; feasting figures and goblets to the dining room; and, wrought from the newel post of the otherwise plain stairs, an eponymous salmon.[9] For all the delicacy — and humour — of the carving, the simple, bold handling of the stair and balustrades matches the general sturdiness in construction already noted in the external rafters. Glasswork also prevailed. Around the stairway small leaded glass lights incorporate geometrical flower forms, climaxing in a twin-light elongated feature in the attic games-room. The kitchen wall originally contained a stained glass panel depicting a meal of fish and excerpts from Burns's *A Cotter's Saturday Night*. The total combines to give a very gay, personal warmth of touch without reducing the design to an indulgence.

As work on the Mercantile Chambers and Rowantreehill drew to a close, Salmon began design work for another group of office chambers for a Mr James Miller, at 142a-144 St Vincent Street, Glasgow, 1898-99. The site, in contrast to that for the Mercantile Chambers, was a mere 29 feet 6 inches (8.9metres) wide and 109 feet (33.2metres) deep, with limited boundary access at the narrow front and rear restricting daylight rights. The resulting office was laid out on an irregular dumb-bell plan with light wells on either side of a narrow 'neck' to allow natural daylight to the chambers in the centre of the building.[10] To achieve the maximum amount of glazed area to the street front, Salmon used a cantilevered steel frame construction to carry the loads from the façade and the floors back to H-section columns located entirely within the building. The elevation therefore carried no structural weight, which allowed the stonework to be whittled to the minimum, thereby permitting the glazing to be held within a thin skeletal stone frame. The composition of the front elevation is based on three interlocking bays. Two oriel bays run the height of the building and a centre bay alternately recedes and protrudes, ensuring no two floors of the building are the same. The sculpture is sinuous and 'molten', focused in a variety of delicate, sometimes precious, highlights: filigree strands of tiny beads sit between bolder ogee pediments; atop the horseshoe doorways, satyrs support the oriel lanterns; and above the shop level, little flying lanterns, perhaps mimicking the overall building form, enmesh together with figures and tree limb forms. The sculpture and ogee pediments reduce as the building rises and the design is finished off with a part-octagonal tower with contrasting concave and convex curves to the attic window finials, the pinnacles adding to its lively free spirit and providing its affectionate *sobriquet* of 'The Hatrack'. The flowing curves of the carved external forms are carried throughout the design to include the ogee and 'onion' forms of the wrought iron work around the lift cage, stairway rails and rooftop railings, which all add to the dynamic restlessness of the building. The stained glass in the lantern above the entrance has been attributed to Oscar Paterson and comprises the form of a ship in strong rich colours, generally warm and dark in tone. The wall tiling to the hall areas was originally a mix of dark blue and deep green, adding a mystical northern air. The rear elevation borrows the canted bay forms of the Mercantile Chambers but the lead spandrel panels of the former are here replaced with roughcast and the windows are recessed to create a play on solid and void, perhaps foiling with that of the front elevation.

As the front stonework has been reduced to a minimum, so structure and ornament have become more integrated. The handling of the sculpture in its gradual release from the stonework is developed from the earlier fish carving and arch-springing details on the Mercantile Chambers. It includes here the stone

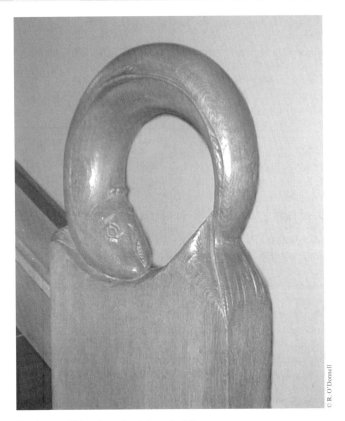

The signatory 'Salmon' newel post, Rowantreehill.

Pilaster incorporating a carving of the Earth, Rowantreehill.

Titular entrance-hall pilaster incorporating an elf and a rowan tree, Rowantreehill.

column and elongated lintel arrangement previously noted and also the carved features such as ogee pediments, lanterns, bay-window cornices, column bases and curled extruded eyelets. The carving is 'of' the building and not 'on' the building, much of it being blended and dressed *in situ* and not remotely in a studio. As these features release themselves from the stonework, the elevation appears to become a rippling decorated mass on a glass façade, apparently shifting and moving with the changes of light and shade. The effects are further enhanced by the windows, which were originally top-hung and accordingly had no intervening sashes. This omitted any distracting cross-rails and, as the glass filled the void, emphasised the visual dynamic between the glass and the stone. The plastic quality of the sculpture, apparently emerging from a vertical water surface, the glass, suggests the

St Vincent Chambers, 142a-144
St Vincent Street, Glasgow,
1898-99, photographed *c*.1906.
*The Builders' Journal And
Architectural Engineer,* 1906.

Interconnecting bays to front elevation, St Vincent Chambers.

hand of Francis Derwent Wood once again.[11] Wood had been
awarded the Gold Medal at the Royal Academy Schools in 1896
for his study of *Daedalus and Icarus,* and this piece and other
work by him, such as *Baby's Head,* were formally similar to the
work of Rodin in their use of lifting, rising and merging forms.

A contemporary critical review of the building denounced this
treatment in the stone carving, noting 'Mr Salmon's offices are
unmistakably "new art" and at least the technical execution may be
praised ... [but] ... the architectural quality is poor; stone is treated
as if a plastic material, and generally the forms are capricious for
all materials. This disregard of convention in architecture is just as
inartistic as a natural treatment of ornament without
conventionalism is'.[12] The Glasgow sculptor Albert Hodge, whom
the firm employed on other projects, also objected to this

Satyr feature over entrance, St Vincent Chambers.

Lift cage ironwork with distinctive 'onion' motif, St Vincent Chambers.

treatment of stone carving, announcing that 'to obtain the best architectural results our work must have decided outlines, and any tendency to lose it in the background be guarded against ... Modern French work looks as if it were clay modeling'.[13] John Ruskin had earlier noted 'The essential thing in a building—its *first* virtue — is that it be strongly built, and fit for its uses. The noblest thing in a building, and its *highest* virtue, is that it be nobly sculptured'.[14] The sculptural treatment of 'The Hatrack' is central to the architectural expression created by Salmon and requires discussion.

Little is known of Wood's own artistic philosophy but the physical treatment of the semi-submerged or re-emerging forms in

Naturalistic forms of stair balustrading, St Vincent Chambers.

his work was used by both Auguste Rodin, whose work he would have known at first hand, and Michelangelo Buonarroti (1475-1564), whose work he would have studied. Michelangelo, like Salmon, envisaged the universe engulfed in a constant process of destruction and renewal, and the problems of an individual soul of interest only insofar as they partook in the cosmic sequence of 'death and resurrection'.[15] He was steeped in Neo-Platonic thought which was expressed in his poetry and art, not only in the finished piece, but also in his method of physically realising it. He viewed an unworked marble block as containing an image or figure within it, and the rôle of the sculptor to be that of 'breaking the marble spell'.[16] He would begin carving from what would be the principal face of the finished work and peel 'the figure out of the prison of the stone'.[17] The artist, critic and biographer Giorgio Vasari (1511-1574) described the process in this way. Consider a figure lying in a horizontal position in a bath being slowly raised out of the water. First would emerge the most protruding parts, then one would see the figure in relief, and finally the figure in its three-dimensional roundness. The process is confirmed by the unfinished works of *Saint Matthew*, 1506, *Atlas*, 1513-20, and *Awakening Slave*, 1520-23, where the surfaces of the pieces become less finished and worked as the figures retire into the mass of the stone block. Michelangelo often left parts of the finished work unwrought or merging into the unworked base, as seen in *Victory* of the 1530s, and the figures on the tomb of Giuliano de Medici in the Medici Chapel, Florence 1520-34, where the figures remain linked physically and metaphysically to their past and their future, i.e.

The 'softly' carved pilaster eyelets, and elongated lintol and cornice arrangement, St Vincent Chambers.

ashes to ashes, dust to dust.[18]

Auguste Rodin (1840-1917), who studied and greatly admired Michelangelo, recognised the significance of maintaining this link between man's past, present and future, and incorporated the contrasts between wrought and unwrought stone into his own work. He argued that 'no good sculptor can model a human figure without dwelling on the mystery of life; this individual and that in fleeting variations only remind him of the immanent type; he is led perpetually from the creature to the creator ... All the best works of any artist must be bathed, so to speak, in mystery. That is why many of my figures have a hand, a foot still imprisoned in the marble block; life is everywhere, but rarely indeed does it come to

*Baby's Head, c.*1895, Francis Derwent Wood (1871-1926).

complete expression or the individual to perfect freedom'.[19] While works such as *The Danaid,* 1885, *The Muse,* 1900 and *The Secret,* 1910, clearly demonstrate this philosophy, one figure in particular embodies it more than any other. Rodin's *The Earth,* 1884, has been likened by Albert Elsen to 'a gigantic slug, a sub-human species still attached to primordial mud'.[20] The piece suggests the emergence of a life form which remains largely incomplete and appears to be immersed in molten bronze in an ongoing process involving an 'irresistible power, not dependent on muscular energy'.[21] The figure's enactment of generation and its apparent convulsions fully convey Rodin's ideas of the 'mystical correspondences of growth that link all living matter'[22] and tie his philosophy to that of Michelangelo, and Salmon.[23]

While the similarities between the philosophies of the three are obvious, and the significance of the sculptural treatment to their work equally so, how do we know Salmon was in close control of the sculptural process at 'The Hatrack'? It is a matter of record that Salmon was trained in modelling at the Art School and studied and sketched sculpture throughout Europe, including Versailles and Naples. Salmon also (later) recounted the skills of the Dutch sculptor Johan Keller at modelling directly onto a

*Awakening Slave, c.*1520-23 (marble) by Michelangelo Buonarroti (1475-1564).

The Earth, 1884, (bronze S.623) Auguste Rodin (1840-1917).

building, specifically noting that 'reliefs should be such as are naturally modelled in a plastic material'.[24] As he also sketched a design for a figure of St Mungo specifically for 'The Hatrack', and reputedly executed carving work at Rowantreehill, there is little doubt that he would have been fully alert to the significance of the carving process and controlled its marriage with the overall composition.[25] Perhaps reinforcing Ruskin's contention that 'a great architect must be a great sculptor',[26] the aesthetic of 'The Hatrack' was not the result of a preference or chance occurrence consequential on the 'style' or technique of the sculptor acting independently, but was that pursued, sought and controlled by Salmon, the architect-sculptor. Like Michelangelo's figures, Salmon's St Vincent Street Chambers appears to be emerging from a water surface (the glass) and, as Rodin's *The Earth*, gaining its involuntary inertia from some inherent and intrinsic universal energy. In Chicago Louis Sullivan also believed in a 'life force', whose architectural expression depended on the plastic execution of the ornament. While 'ornament is applied in the sense of being

cut in or cut on … it should appear when completed, as though by the out working of some beneficent agency, that it had come forth from the very substance of the material'.[27]

Just as the sculptural treatment sat uncomfortably with his contemporaries and critics, so too did the reduction of the stonework to a minimalist rôle with the resulting play on solid and void. In 1892 Mackintosh had cautioned against the presence of a large amount of glazing at ground level because he considered that 'the eye is distressed'.[28] *The Studio* critic W. L. Watson later directly criticised Salmon, noting that 'in certain structural details due regard is not paid to the appearance of stability, and there is occasionally an absence of that tranquilising impression of perfect safety'.[29] In 'The Hatrack' Salmon appears to have been oblivious to these concerns. While Burnet and Campbell felt it necessary to visually 'stop' the Athenaeum at ground level with two windows punctuating a rusticated base, Salmon allowed the glass-stone combination of 'The Hatrack' to drift between the ground and basement levels, maximising the incongruity of the steeply sloping

St Vincent Chambers, 142a-144 St Vincent Street, Glasgow. This 2003 photograph illustrates the transformatory dimension of the building. To the east (rhs), stone predominates over glass in Burnet, Boston & Carruthers' offices at no. 142, 1899-1900. In the middle, Salmon maximises the 'void' over 'solid' relationship, with glass predominating over stone. To the west (lhs), glass is all embracing in King, Main, & Ellison's Scottish Amicable Life Assurance office, 1973-76.

RCAHMS

site.[30] Overall, the office is more reminiscent of the flowing Art Nouveau compositions of Henri Van de Velde, Victor Horta, Hector Guimard and Antoní Gaudí, than the starker Glasgow Style work of C. R. Mackintosh and J. Gibb Morton.[31]

The play on solid and void, stone and glass, and between flat surface and raised motif are the keys to the building's expression. Salmon emphasised verticality by the use of bay windows as Burnet and Campbell had done at the Athenaeum. But by also utilising mouldings derived from Leiper along with sculptural techniques taken from the Continent, in combination with the technical possibilities offered by structural steel, he created a work of architecture entirely new in expression.

By the time the building was completed in 1899 the practice had undergone a major reorganisation. In recognition of his growing contribution to the office, Forrest Salmon made Gillespie his partner in 1897—although his name did not appear in the firm's title until 1903. In 1898, after completing his formal qualifications as an architect, James also became a partner and the firm took on a new young apprentice, William Alexander Kidd, who would become an important figure to the practice in later years.[32]

Johan Keller (1863-1944) et al. *The Bailie*, 1907.

'A friend is, as it were, a second self'.

Marcus Tillius Cicero, *De Amicitia*

'Friendship needs a certain parallelism of life, a community of thought, a rivalry of aim'.

Henry Adams, *The Education of Henry Adams,* 1918

ARCHITECTURAL ANALYSIS:
SALMON AND GILLESPIE: A DIFFERENCE IN TASTES

The Marine Hotel, Troon, built 1897.

Front entrance detail, The Marine Hotel.

While Salmon had been committed to the Mercantile Chambers and 'The Hatrack', Gillespie was engaged on the Marine Hotel, Troon, 1897; the British Linen Bank at Govan Cross, Glasgow, also 1897; and the design of the St Andrew's Free Church Halls at 685 Alexandra Parade, Glasgow, 1898. The Marine Hotel is located on the Clyde coast, immediately facing the famous golf links of Royal Troon. Designed on a symmetrical E-plan with a three gable front elevation of red sandstone, each gable has arched windows which gradually diminish in prominence up to the third and attic levels by a reduction in glazed area and fenestration, and are topped by an ogee-shaped crown similar to that at the earlier British Linen Bank, High Street, Glasgow, 1894-96. While the external elevations in their simplicity recall the work of the English Arts and Crafts designers, internally the debt was even more obvious. The large hall was originally plainly treated in oak and effect was achieved 'by the proportion and effective distribution of spaces'[1] as opposed to the use of 'insignificant ornamentation'.[2] Decoration was limited to wrought gargoyle forms on the truss ends of the billiard room rafters which contrasted with an overall starkness. The smaller rooms shared 'the same sobriety of treatment',[3] and a 'harmony [existed]

between room and furniture ... due ... to the fact that [both had been] designed by the architects of the building'.[4] Following this building, Gillespie designed the British Linen Bank, 816-18 Govan Road, Govan Cross, Glasgow, 1897. The building is located at an important main street corner site, which Gillespie emphasised by the location of the main entrance below a very individual octagonal tower, capped with a daringly free and lively 'crown of thorns' in lead. Flanked by tall chimney-pieces, the

RCAHMS

The Billiard Room at The Marine Hotel, showing the carved truss ends and simple detailing, photographed by Annan, *c.*1902.

© R. O'Donnell

The British Linen Bank, Govan Cross, Glasgow, built 1897-98.

corner tower and entrance are further elaborated by sculptured features in the form of an emerging ship's bow and flanking winged angel figures. The two street-front elevations have ground floor arched windows and are similar in overall composition to the Marine Hotel. Again gradation is the major compositional tool, but instead of relying for effect solely on the reduction of window area with height, on the east elevation the curvaceous ogee window pediments appear to withdraw back onto the stone elevation from ground to upper floors and then ultimately 'eat' into the stone surface. This effect is juxtaposed with the swelling form of an ogee 'dome' to the adjacent bay window, the restless, active effect highlighted by the absence of framing lines or other ornamentation to the curving form. The modulated effect is achieved by a similar sculptural treatment to that employed by Salmon at the Mercantile Chambers and 'The Hatrack', and again suggests the hand of Derwent Wood, this time working in collaboration with the Dutch sculptor Johan Keller (1863-1944).[5] The oriental ogee shape, by now a favourite motif of both Salmon and Gillespie, is once more evident in the treatment of the window pediments. The elevations are stopped emphatically by a strong horizontal line at roof level, effected by a very bold eaves overhang. The truss ends are exposed in a Japanese manner, and supported at intermediate points by curved timber brackets resting on plain square stone blocks which protrude from the wall face. The overhanging eaves are in turn

© R. O'Donnell

Dramatic wrought angel figures and ship above the entrance of the British Linen Bank, Govan Cross.

framed by elongated vertical flanking chimneys and the central corner turret. There is a general feeling of restraint (and containment) in the composition although the gay corner crown, foiling against the simplicity of the main elevations, does lift its mood.

Gillespie's more restrained 'crafts approach' continued in his design for church halls at 685 Alexandra Parade, Glasgow, 1898.

© R. O'Donnell

Diminishing pediment treatment, and swollen carved bay capping to the east elevation of the British Linen Bank, Govan Cross.

The Mitchell Library, Cultural and Leisure Services

St Andrew's Free Church Hall, 685 Alexandra Parade, Glasgow, 1898: perspective drawing by John Gaff Gillespie. *The British Architect,* 1902.

© R. O'Donnell

Art Nouveau influenced detail to iron fencing, St Andrew's Free Church Halls.

© R. O'Donnell

Angel figures above entrance, St Andrew's Free Church Halls.

Lloyd Morris Congregational Church, 155-197 Rutherglen Road, Glasgow, 1901: perspective drawing by John Gaff Gillespie. *Glasgow Advertiser and Property Circular*, 1901.

The accommodation required was minimal, consisting of the hall itself, a vestry and toilets. This resulted in a simple plan with elevations in a similar style to those of old Scottish Reformation churches such as fifteenth century Fordell. The hall has a large roof area with a wide over-sailing eaves, apparently weighing down on the walls tucked underneath. The windows have four-centered arches, with the entrance and the extent of accommodation denoted by two squat corner towers flanking the line of the eaves. Constructed of blonde sandstone with a slate roof, the simplicity of the building's external appearance is carried into the main hall where the roof trusses were originally exposed, resting on plain stone corbels. At a more detailed level, the external figures and iron railings with sinuous double return lines and thickness variations acknowledge the influence of Continental

Street front elevation of 12 University Gardens, Glasgow, built 1900.

Stained Glass work by Oscar Paterson, 12 University Gardens.

Fireplace detail in entrance hall, 12 University Gardens.

Mosaic feature above first floor fireplace, 12 University Gardens.

Carved figurehead to newel post of stair by John Crawford, 12 University Gardens.

Art Nouveau. Two angels holding between them an open book appear to rise from the stone surface of the west tower, and another elongated winged figure seems to have passed through the stone mantel by a *trompe l'oeil* effect.[6]

Simplicity and Arts and Crafts directness remained Gillespie's trademarks over the next few years and are especially evident in his competition-winning entry for the Lloyd Morris Congregational Church, Rutherglen Road, Glasgow, 1901 (demolished), and a four-storey terrace town house at 12 University Gardens, 1900. The Lloyd Morris Church had a remarkable resemblance to the earlier John MacIntyre Building, University Gardens, 1887-95, by Sir J. J. Burnet, with its topless tower and 'subtle vestigial crenellation'.[7] As at Alexandra Parade, timber trusses were left exposed and unadorned. The detail of the street elevation, however, was entirely unique and original. It had flowing mouldings around the entrance doorway, ogee extruded pediments to the triple window opening, and an ogee cut recess to the double window opening, all within the tower form. Interesting cross-compositional relationships were established between the pedimented dormer windows above the shop and the openings within the body of the tower.[8] Similar multiple relationships between horizontal and vertical elements were later developed by Mackintosh in his revised designs for the west elevation of the Glasgow School of Art, 1905-07.

At 12 University Gardens, Gillespie's hand continued to exercise a close aesthetic control. The elevation is relieved only by a moulding around the doorway, some wrought ironwork at the first floor balcony, the familiar ogee-shaped cap to the turret denoting the entrance, and a very solidly constructed glass panelled front door. Internally the building is handled with a non-period Arts and Crafts simplicity. There are open timber beams, canvas-lined walls with green-stained strapping, a sparing use of ornament to highlight structural details, stained glass features by Oscar Paterson, carved stone fireplaces by Albert Hodge and fitted furniture by John Crawford. Of especial interest are the 'open book' form capitals to the pilasters of the library room door, the dark-stained seating at the entrance hall, and the carved figureheads to the stair newel posts. Also of note are the bold Japanese forms and black colour to the upper level doorhead facings, which particularly recall Mackintosh. The generally subdued atmosphere is distinctly Scottish in its sombreness, and muted through the understatement of the forms and colouring.

In sharp contrast, the previous year the firm completed the first

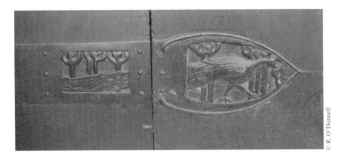

Peacock hinge detail to storm doors of 22 Park Circus, Glasgow, built 1900.

Richly carved fireplace to ground floor Banqueting Room, 22 Park Circus.

Fireplace mosaic by Stephen Adam, 22 Park Circus.

Art Nouveau figure by Francis Derwent Wood 'emerging' from wall panel to ante-room, 22 Park Circus.

RCAHMS

Fireplace incorporating a 'Lantern' display cabinet feature, 22 Park Circus.

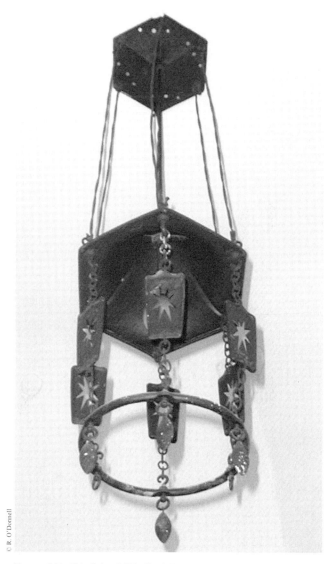

© R. O'Donnell

Entrance lobby light fitting, 14 Woodlands Terrace, Glasgow, built 1902.

Lounge, 14 Woodlands Terrace. Photographed *c.*1902.

View of Hall, 14 Woodlands Terrace. The woodwork was executed by Wylie & Lochead, and the electric fittings and door fingerplates supplied by The Bromsgrove Guild. Photographed *c.*1902.

Main entrance British Linen Bank, Hutchesontown Branch, 162 Gorbals Street, Glasgow, built 1899-1900.

stage of elaborate interior renovations to a house little more than a quarter of a mile away at 22 Park Circus, for the iron goods manufacturer Walter MacFarlane. The internal details could hardly be more ornate and further from simple Arts and Crafts, and it is difficult to imagine Gillespie as the designer in preference to

RCAHMS

Glasgow Style Agents Room, British Linen Bank, Hutchesontown Branch, photographed *c*.1901.

© R. O'Donnell

Balcony ironwork, British Linen Bank, Hutchesontown Branch.

Salmon. The original interior was by James Boucher and richly finished in the style of an Italian palazzo. The new work involved the re-lining of some of the interior paneling, rebuilding of fireplaces and mantels, and the construction of new doors. Salmon's alterations are sympathetic in spirit if not style to Boucher's design. At the entrance double-leaf folding oak storm doors bear carved figures, flanked top and bottom by elaborate pierced leaf-form hinge plates incorporating peacocks that are reminiscent of Celtic brooch imagery. Internally the new fireplaces and mantelpieces are of satinwood, richly carved and inlaid with sinuous Art Nouveau trees, figures and *bon mots* by Derwent Wood. The fireplace in the anteroom incorporates within its multi-layered centrepiece a tile mosaic of two young girls reading a book with the miniature inscription 'I was made by Stephen Adam 1898'.[9] The dreamy figures and colouring strongly recalls the work of David Gauld and the Glasgow Boys. An upstairs fireplace incorporates an ogee-shaped 'lantern' display cabinet, similar to a window design for St Andrew's in the East

Halls; and a built-in seat with figures carved at the arm-rests recalls work at Rowantreehill, Kilmacolm. The rear office rooms (now accessed from Park Street) have paneled walls with delicate inlaid Shakesperean figures in pale timbers, while the ante rooms are in stark contrast being lined in dark timbers, which effect a haunting atmosphere.[10] The light fittings were also designed by Salmon, one example comprising metal discs and chains suspending heart pendants around a central plate of *repoussé* sinuous foliage. The Scottish architectural historian Professor David M. Walker considers the interior carving amongst the finest examples of Art Nouveau in Britain.

The subtle curvaceous forms persisted in Salmon's interior renovations for the Liberal MP, Alec Cross, at 14 and 15

© R. O'Donnell

Stylised ironwork to back-court stairs, British Linen Bank, Hutchesontown Branch.

The Mitchell Library, Cultural and Leisure Services

Art Nouveau archway for the Glasgow International Exhibition, 1901. Commissioned and executed by John Crawford, designed by Salmon. *The Art Journal,* 1901.

Woodlands Terrace, Glasgow, 1902,[11] for which he also designed light fittings. Although now substantially destroyed, contemporary photographs reveal thin twisted corinthianesque columns at the over-mantel, parabolic arched recesses at the fireplace, and a metal-disc and chain combination to the lights once again. Of particular interest is the absence of a cornice where the wall and ceilings meet, the two surfaces being allowed to curve seamlessly into each other. Externally the door at number 14 (which is still intact) has characteristically bold curved and coloured glass sections set in a mahogany frame and screen, and wrought metal

finger plates to the locks incorporating a 'Glasgow' rose. An aquatic figure again appears, creating the horizontal stroke of the number '4.'

From a slightly earlier period is the design of the British Linen Company Bank's Hutchesontown branch, which although plain in composition originally contained a fine Glasgow style interior of dark timber paneling with matching fittings and furniture. Sadly now abandoned, only the remains of the fine swirling ironwork at the front balcony and rear stairs, and the characteristic arch springing, hint at the quality of the original detail.

79 West Regent Street, Glasgow, 1900-04; perspective drawing by John Gaff Gillespie. *The Builders' Journal and Architectural Record,* 1904.

Glasgow Savings Bank, 756 Argyle Street, Anderston Cross, Glasgow, built 1899-1900.

A distinctive hall archway design commissioned by John Crawford, the artisan wood carver, followed in 1901 for the Glasgow International Exhibition. In the characteristic European horse-shoe form it had flanking integral elongated columns that transformed into framing voids at their intersection with the arch. The arc itself swept down to finish with carved Celtic figureheads, and up to the apex where two scrolls engaged clasp-like, effecting a play on solid and void. A central panel carried the maxim 'the life so short, the art so long to learn', a variation on the Latin *ars longa vita brevis*, and a panel to the bottom right recorded that the

Copper panel with Glasgow Style 'Lion Rampant', 79 West Regent Street.

Rich mosaic entrance semi-dome and delicate carved entwining leaf forms, Glasgow Savings Bank, Anderson Cross.

RCAHMS

simplicity in design but that he 'here entered into the spirit of the exhibitor',[12] to allow Crawford to display the abilities of his craftsmen. Following the Glasgow show, Francis Newbery selected the piece for exhibitions in Turin and Budapest in 1902.

The characteristic elongated forms and curves are again evident at 79 West Regent Street, Glasgow, 1900-04. This office renovation involved the formation of a rear extension that was carried out using similar canted forms to those at St Vincent Street Chambers, and new bay windows to the front elevation developed from the Mercantile Chambers. The latter are lined with beaten relief copper panels depicting the coats of arms of Glasgow and Scotland at ground level, and the initials of the architects, builders and client at first floor level, all in a highly characteristic Glasgow Style manner.

The overall oval frames are crossed through at the top by a curved rectilinear 'sub-frame' that elongates to become Celtic dragon-like(?) heads for the city's coat of arms and a truncated triangular 'medal' for the country's coat of arms. While the forms have an elusive meandering quality their subtle blending from out of the flat metal plain adds to their mystique. The expression achieved is similar to that created by the sculptor's hand in the stone carving on 'The Hatrack'.

By the end of 1900 the firm had executed what was to be their last major new bank commission, the Glasgow Savings Bank, 756 Argyle Street, Anderston Cross, to designs by Gillespie. The planning and overall form of the building is similar to his earlier Govan Cross Bank, but the detailing of the stone-carved features is extremely intricate and ornate, and more reminiscent of Leiper, suggesting a possible design input by Salmon. The building is a bolder design than the previous Govan Cross bank, being composed of dramatic isolated elements as opposed to graduated ones, and recalls the compositional approach adopted for the Mercantile Chambers. Of particular interest is the spectacular door piece sculpted by Albert Hodge with delicate figure carvings, entwining leaf forms and a blue Venetian glass mosaic semi-dome. The pilasters to the gabled corner dome have flower and stem forms grouped to create capitals. Ogee pediments are again prevalent and an interesting introduction is the horizontally proportioned upper sashes of the windows, never before present on any of the firm's buildings. The winged and hooded angel figures to the external walls, turret and bank hall fireplace are all carried out in the very distinctive elongated Glasgow Style.

Although Gillespie claimed responsibility for the design, both partners may have had a hand in it, and certainly they exchanged

work was executed by Crawford to a design by Salmon. The columns were entirely original, incorporating wrought figures at the capitals, four flanking pilotis at the bases and molten carved pedestals. The overall impression is that of tree forms branching upwards into the voids above the line of the curve. The spiritual expression of the design is mysterious, and its symbolism and multiple criss-crossing lines recall Celtic jewel imagery. There is also an heroic Aryan quality in the smoothness of the idealised figureheads, similar to the spirit found in Hoffmann's work. *The Art Journal* interestingly notes that Salmon's preference is for

Corner gabled dome with capitals created by grouped flower forms, Glasgow Savings Bank, Anderston Cross.

Corner detail showing winged and hooded angel figures, Glasgow Savings Bank, Anderston Cross.

ideas. While preparing preliminary schemes, Salmon drew the St Vincent Street Chambers with a crown of thorns cap taken from Gillespie's Govan Cross bank; equally, the stables built at the Marine Hotel as part of the extension work carried out in 1900 display detail characteristics usually associated with Salmon.

The question of authorship is also raised when considering a design for a combined electric fire and clock in beaten brass, which was exhibited in Glasgow in 1901, and in Turin in 1902. This was in an idiosyncratic Glasgow Style incorporating bird, tree and fish motifs — perhaps announcing its native city origins — and organic climbing vine forms. It was attributed to Gillespie in the catalogue accompanying the exhibition in Turin, but the

design's elaborate elongated surface delineation, ogee and extenuated capital forms, arched backdrop and 'spookish' character, are all distinctively Salmonesque. Indeed, Salmon's known interest in internal features and electrical lighting, and most particularly the signatory aquatic figures below the clock bell and flanking the saintly figure (St Francis?), all point to his influence. It is again feasible, of course, that both worked on the project. The background scene was painted by G. G. Anderson, a friend of William Forrest Salmon, and the plaster frieze was carried out by Albert Hodge. The flanking lights were open orbs made from curved metal straps, and are likely to have also been designed by the firm. Salmon's interest in lighting saw him later develop a

Salmon's perspective drawing of 1899 showing the St Vincent Chambers with a crown-of-thorns cap. *The Builders' Journal and Architectural Record,* 1902.

The Mitchell Library, Cultural and Leisure Services

RCAHMS

Photograph *c.*1900 of the stables to The Marine Hotel, shows extended eaves details, and rafter ends cut in the form of open mouthed fish — all very similar to Salmon's Rowantreehill.

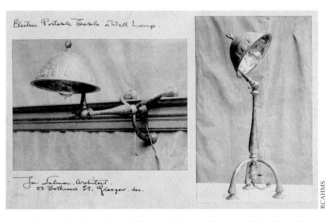

RCAHMS

Design for a reading lamp that could be used either standing on a table, or hung from a dado rail.

combined table/wall lamp with tripod base and adjustable head, and an adjustable illumination system he grandly entitled 'Aero Electroliers' in 1912.[13]

While both men's designs were in the Glasgow Style — common features of their work being the use of ogee forms, elongated sinuous lines, naturalistic features, the exploration of carved effects, solid to void relationships and elaboration of ornament — Salmon's were free and lively compositions depending on elaborate sculptured features and superb artistry. By contrast, Gillespie's designs were more subdued, less intensely detailed and decorated, relying more for effect on supreme craftsmanship and focusing on subtle highlighted features. However both approaches, the Art Nouveau and the Arts and Crafts, shared a common dependence on the skill of the artisan for their realisation.

Perhaps the difference between the two men is best illustrated by

Glasgow Style electric fire and clock in beaten brass, designed 1901.

their choice of sculptors. Francis Derwent Wood, who used molten forms in his work, predominantly worked on Salmon's buildings, only contributing the ornate corner feature to Gillespie's bank at Govan Cross. Albert Hodge, who believed in defined lines and abhorred 'Modern French work',[14] i.e. Art Nouveau, was never employed on any of the buildings attributed to Salmon, only those claimed by Gillespie. We know that ideas were exchanged between Salmon and Gillespie, but exactly to what extent can never be certain.

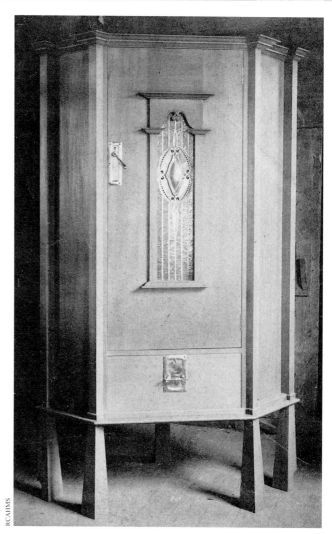

Corner wardrobe in cypress wood, designed c.1900.

'Houses are built to live in, not to look on.'

Francis Bacon, *Essay 45 — Of Building*

'A house is a machine for living in.'

Le Corbusier, *Vers une Architecture (Towards an Architecture)*

ARCHITECTURAL ANALYSIS: SIMPLICITY AND THE HOUSES

Salmon's preference for simplicity in design, noted in the review of the Glasgow Exhibition of 1901, began to manifest itself increasingly in the early years of the new century. A competition design for Newton Park School, Ayr, 1902, relied on simple geometries and forms, with white roughcast walls. Although ogee forms persisted in the roof sections and main roof ventilator, it is the formal clarity of the buildings that creates the strongest impression, perhaps best illustrated in the reduction of the janitor's house to a basic octagon (which by its siting allowed supervision of all the gateways and boundaries similar to the principle of the 'Panopticon').

Salmon next designed the very plain nurses' home and pathological wing at Woodilee Asylum, Lenzie in 1904. The building is a simple brick block, planned as a series of graduated

Front view of Nurses Home and Pathological Block, Woodilee Asylum, Lenzie, designed 1904.

Rear view of Nurses Home and Pathological Block, Woodilee Asylum, Lenzie.

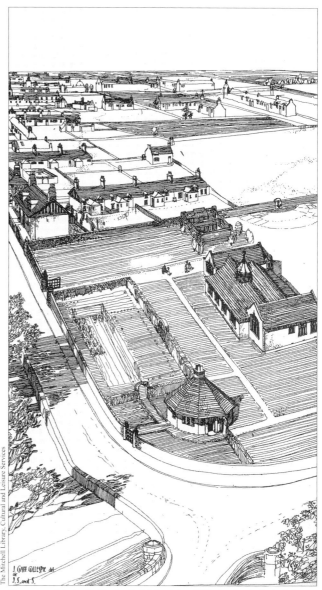

The proposed design for Newton Park School, Ayr, 1902, showing the janitor's house. The octagon form appeared time and again in Salmon's work. *The British Architect*, 1902.

Chauffeur's House and Garage, Gallowhill, Paisley, 1903. *The Architectural Review,* 1903.

Lanfine Cottage Hospital for Consumptives, Broomhill, Kirkintilloch, 1904: perspective drawing by John Gaff Gillespie. *The Builders' Journal and Architectural Record,* 1904.

pavilion forms with no external decoration, and has a sedate character when compared to the previous designs for offices. The only stylistic nuances are again at roof level where deep overhanging eaves, pinnacled ventilators, hooded dormers, and a raised and curving centre section create interest.

During this time Gillespie continued his understated approach when designing a chauffeur's house and garage for Gallowhill House (designed by Forrest Salmon), Paisley (demolished). Like Salmon at Rowantreehill, Gillespie adopted a mix of timber frame and white roughcast wall construction in combination with a deep exposed eaves overhang, but unlike Rowantreehill there was little whimsical decoration and the overall impression was calmer. The composition was generally asymmetrical, the Arts and Crafts rawness relieved only by dressed and buttressed stonework around the entrance, part-arches over the windows, an ogee cover to the roof ventilator, and an idiosyncratic tapered stone capping to the roughcast chimneys. The strong corner pylon stopping the line of the roof eaves recalled the earlier St Andrew's in the East Church Halls.

Gillespie next designed the plain, white roughcast Lanfine Cottage Hospital for Consumptives, Broomhill, Kirkintilloch, 1904. Simpler than the chauffeur's house at Gallowhill, the hospital comprises two wings to an L-shaped plan linked by a squat square central block. Although quite plain, the square dormers which align with the windows below the eaves of the verandah create an interesting effect, whereby a series of internal volumes appear to be passing through the slope of the roof.

At the end of 1904 Salmon designed his second house in Kilmacolm, Miyanoshita. In contrast to Rowantreehill, it presented a modest but distinguished frontage following a rectilinear plan elevated uniformly over three storeys to roof level. Mackintosh's Windyhill — built on the site adjacent to Rowantreehill two years after its completion — may well have been an influence for its

Miyanoshita, Porterfield Road, Kilmacolm, built 1904.

The tendril-like supported light, and simple and distinguished entrance to Miyanoshita.

The carved putteé to the side of the entrance, Miyanoshita.

severity and simplicity, as Salmon would have been able to observe it at very close proximity. Constructed of snecked rubble with a slate roof, the plainness of Miyanoshita is relieved only by small infant figures carved on either side of the entrance and an Art Nouveau light bracket. The figures, as at 'The Hatrack', would have been partially carved on site as they are not wrought from a single block but each comprise three stones coursed and dressed to marry with the ashlar. Internally, isolated features, such as the glazed entrance wall, ingleneuks, corner fireplaces 'enriched with Delft-tiling',[1] and elongated parabolic arch recesses, provide the main relief. The stair is again strongly modeled but strictly confined. An interesting spatial effect is created with the first floor

bedroom walls, which are allowed to merge seamlessly with the ceilings to create a 'barrel-vault' like effect, mirroring that at Woodlands Terrace. The rich flowing features of his earlier work are less evident and his approach is more reserved than severe, and bears a closer affinity to Arts and Crafts simplicity and economy. Some of the furniture was provided by William Stewart Morton (Scott Morton's son and James's cousin), and appears to have included a very individual *japanesque* occasional table. Although there is a general feeling of containment effected by the tightness and rigidity of the plan, relief can be achieved by opening up the partitions between the dining room, inner hall and drawing room to create a 55 foot 'long gallery' which provides fine views to the

Den O'Gryffe, off Knockbuckle Road, Kilmacolm, 1905-06. The drawing was submitted to the local Dean of Guild authority.

Renfrewshire hills. Salmon also laid out the gardens, selecting the plants, shrubs, trees and their placement. Professor Frank A. Walker has noted a rugged romanticism to the landscaping, effected by the heavy stone retaining walls piled up to contain the natural topography.

Following Miyanoshita the firm embarked on a two-year period designing and building a series of domestic commissions, including three houses and two house extensions in Kilmacolm, one house in Giffnock near Glasgow, and one house in Edzell. The first of these works is sited near the River Gryffe in Kilmacolm

and was designed for a Mr R. M. Thorne in 1905. Like Miyanoshita, Den O'Gryffe has a simple rectilinear plan and pitched gable roof, but it is constructed of brick walls, white roughcast, and has a red-tiled roof with a broad oversailing eaves. There are small functionally located vertical casements gathered together in horizontal groups with horizontal sashes similar to those at the Anderson Cross bank, and a small picturesque verandah. Inside, the ceiling joists, lintels and doors are all exposed stained timber, and there is no ornamentation or decoration of any kind. The only relief to the starkness of the interiors are dark blue hand-made tiles (Dutch?) around the corner fireplaces, each one arranged in a unique pattern. The reduction of the design to a basic white block suggests a gradual rationalisation process taking place and recalls the work of C. F. A. Voysey, even including the latter's preference for rainwater butts.

This process continued in Salmon's next design for a two-storey extension to an existing house called Northernhay, again in Kilmacolm. Constructed of the same materials used for the original house — roughcast walls, slate roof, exposed timber rafters — it is identifiable from the existing building by the engaged part-octagon corner bay windows that define its extent. While internally there is some fine wood carving in the entrance hall and around the fireplaces, in general, simplicity and directness are the keys to the detailing.[2] Of particular interest externally are the curved window mouldings which can also be seen on 'The Hatrack' light-well windows, and have their origins in Scottish medieval castles.

Between 1905 and 1906 Salmon built a house in Edzell for his maternal aunt, Miss Margaret Alexander. North Lodge adopts the style of Old Scots work, drawing inspiration from nearby Edzell Castle and its garden-wall house for the chimney cappings, roll-mouldings and arched door-pediment. It is constructed of the local red sandstone characteristic of Angus, and incorporates boulders taken from the River North Esk into the walls that give it a rustic quality, and a native texture and colour. Internally the stairs are again bold and plainly wrought, and the walls are lined with canvas rather than wallpaper, which Salmon detested. Of particular interest is the simple, square, geometrical outbuilding with pyramid roof.

Designs for a house called Dilkush (now named Hazelhope) in Kilmacolm, and one called Bolfrax in Glasgow, followed in 1906. Both buildings have red-tiled roofs with extended eaves, and a combination of Tudor style timber-framed walls and roughcast, which formally identify separate areas of the buildings. A minimum of carved stonework enhances the importance of the entrances, that to Dilkush being arched, sweeping and buttressed — and somewhat ecclesiastical — in its repose, while that to Bolfrax incorporates a Tudor pointed arch and is more formal. While both continue an economic approach through the clarity of their construction, an air of whimsy exists in Dilkush. Laid out on an L-shape plan and elevated to varying ridge levels, the different materials of construction, dormers, and variety of window forms, produces interesting geometries and juxtapositions of texture and pattern. The decorative influence of Art Nouveau lingers on in the

Professor F. A. Walker

Detail showing the octagonal treatment of the corners and the window roll moulding to the extension of Northernhay.

drawing room's carved ingleneuk mantel, seats, and cupboards, and a touch of fickleness prevails which recalls Rowantreehill. Bolfrax, although likewise L-shaped in plan, is not as irregular at roof level. There is a pitched gable over the entrance but no dormers, and the building exudes a quiet dignity through its simpler handling and high setting. Internally the walls were

The garden-wall house at Edzell Castle, Angus, which provided inspiration for the roll mouldings, chimneys and arch-pedimented door at North Lodge.

RCAHMS

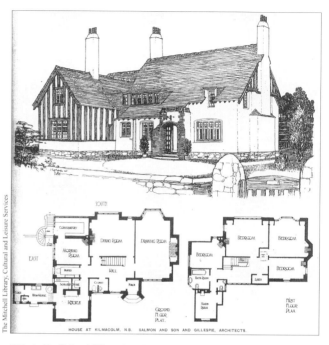

Principal elevation to North Lodge. Boulders were taken from the River North Esk and built into the wall fabric.

originally left at the second coat of plaster and covered with canvas, and the ceiling joists and deafening boards were left exposed and stained. The only relief was provided by plaster panels depicting scenes of *The Hunt,* modeled in the frieze of the living room.

Definitive authorship for these designs is not entirely clear and it is possible that both partners were involved as the mix of construction to the buildings recall Salmon at Rowantreehill, and Gillespie at Gallowhill chauffeur's house and garage. However it is difficult to conceive that Gilllespie would have had a major rôle with Dilkush when it was to be built in Kilmacolm, even though it lacks the 'rustic' economy and general simplicity in overall form of Salmon's Myanoshita, Den O'Gryffe, Northernhay and North Lodge. Likewise it is not clear that Salmon would have been dominant as regards to Bolfrax, given it was sited within a few miles of Gillespie's home and he would surely have supervised it on site. There is perhaps an additional factor. The chief draughtsman Willie Kidd worked with both partners, and specifically assisted on Lanfine Cottage Hospital, 1902-04, and a cottage in Kilmacolm, 1906-07 — which could only have been Dilkush from these dates.[3] The presence of shared details between these buildings, including square dormers and flattened arch windows, may well have occurred almost 'naturally' as a direct result of personnel cross-working and interacting with, and between, Salmon and Gillespie.

Salmon's focus on form persists in an extension to Den

Dilkush, Gryffe Road, Kilmacolm, 1906: perspective drawing by John Gaff Gillespie. *The Builders' Journal and Architectural Engineer,* 1907.

Bolfrax, 224 Fenwick Road, Giffnock, Glasgow, 1906: perspective drawing by John Gaff Gillespie. *The British Architect,* 1907.

Salmon's 1908 sketch of Den O'Gryffe, shows the separation between the old and new provided by the black and white half-timbered link.

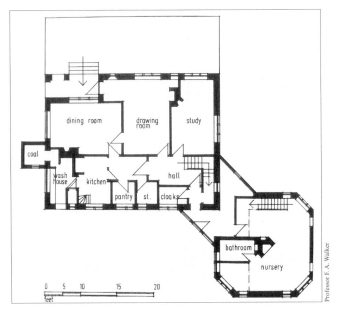

Plan, Den O'Gryffe.

O'Gryffe, with the simple geometry of the Newton Park School janitor's house providing a formal reference point. Salmon made no effort to integrate the new extension into the main house, allowing the two-storey octagonal wing to stand in formal isolation from the existing building, but tied to it by a half-timbered link set at a 45 degree angle to both. The vigour of the composition is heightened by the contrast of the black and white timbering of the link with the white roughcast of the rectangle and octagon of the old and new living spaces. Here again Professor Frank A. Walker has highlighted how the formal integrity of the existing building is thus maintained and that of the new extension reinforced by the juxtaposition of both shapes and materials. The formal contrasts between the old and new work are subservient to unifying horizontal lines established by the ridge of the original house being tied with that of the new wing, the level of the new eaves being aligned with that of the existing dormer, and the horizontal window astragals and groupings of the original house being repeated in the extension. The deep overhanging eaves detail of the original is not repeated in the extension, Salmon preferring to keep the gutter line close to the wall-face, thereby reinforcing the geometrical solidity of the block. Salmon also set a new entrance within the link, which led to spatial incongruities being created between the two living spaces. He capitalised on these awkward spaces by locating a characteristically bold stair within the new hall area, which in turn became a complicated space full of level changes and visual surprises, indeed 'functional opportunity wed to formal complexity'.[4] There is something of

Mackintosh in the changing views through the stair balustrades, and surprise and anticipation experienced as one's shifting position reveals another 'scene'. The simplicity of the external forms is mirrored in the economy of the interior finishes, where 'there are no mouldings, V-joints, beads nor arches'.[5] All the details are notable for their clarity and lack of elaboration.

In 1907 Salmon was commissioned to design a house for a Kilmacolm lawyer, Archibald Ferguson.[6] Again built of brick roughcast walls with a red-tiled roof and heavy exposed rafters, Nether Knockbuckle consists of three modules graded in plan area and volume. The largest module is three storeys high and contains the family reception rooms and bedrooms, the second module is single-storey and contains the kitchen and servants' areas, and the third module, also single-storey, contains the wash-house and pantry. Salmon emphasises the individual shapes of these units, not only in plan and section, but also at a detail level. The extent of the family unit is denoted by two massive angular buttressed chimneys over the end gables, one of which separates this unit from the second module. Similarly a third chimney, smaller in size again, emphasises the independence of the second unit from the third. The chimneystacks themselves are punctuated by narrow slit

View from the east, Nether Knockbuckle, off Florence Drive, Kilmacolm, photographed by Annan, *c.*1908.

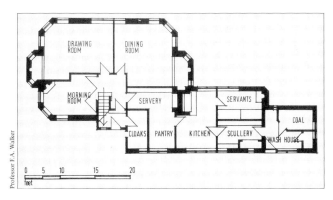

Plan illustrating the modular nature of Nether Knockbuckle.

lights, which adds to their impact. The chamfered corners of the largest module helps to reinforce the heavy eaves and the featureless solid geometry of the whole composition.[7] This is further emphasized by the rafters which are cut perpendicularly to the roof slope and carry V-shaped bespoke gutter sections. Internally, ingleneuks and tile-decorated corner fireplaces are again important features and, as at Den O'Gryffe, no elaborate carving or ornamentation is present. Simplicity is again the key.

This design and the extension to Den O'Gryffe are the maturing results of Salmon's more rational approach to design and his development of the use of basic geometrical forms. The principal elements of the designs each have their own clearly defined identity but are related one to the other both in form and detail to provide unified structures. The unifying horizontal emphasis and juxtaposition of materials and forms has been considered by Professor David M. Walker to suggest an 'awareness of the Chicago School',[8] particularly at Den O'Gryffe. This link would become more pronounced later, with his angular garage and chauffeur's house in Peebles.[9]

Nether Knockbuckle, Kilmacolm.

This exploration of geometry continued in a competition entry for the new Liberal Club at the north-east corner of St George's Place, Glasgow, 1907. It is stylistically a complete departure from the earlier chambers and, perhaps ironically, communicates a domineering power. The basic form of the scheme is that of a cube, with bay windows protruding between the openings of a Corinthian arcade. The bay windows at each end of the Buchanan Street elevation rise through the height of the building slicing through a colossal Doric frieze and deep overhanging cornice which recall J. A. Campbell's offices at 157-67 Hope Street, 1902. Although Salmon emphasised the basic geometrical form of the building and developed the use of the canted bay windows, the substantial mass sitting on top of a two-storey rusticated base has little in common with his earlier works. The compositional variety of arches and columns, bay windows and heavy eaves cornice aligns more with the work of Burnet and Campbell in Glasgow and Louis Sullivan in Chicago, than the plastic articulation of 'The Hatrack'. The design explores the impact of the cubic form, but is not simplistic in its articulation. Perhaps there is some relationship with Sullivan's design for the National Farmers' Bank, Owatonna, 1906-08, which also explored the compositional treatment of a basic geometrical form — and which Salmon later specifically complimented. Although the depth of Salmon's knowledge of Sullivan at this time is not clear, there is conclusive evidence that he was familiar with American architecture and culture — and critical of both. Given that Sullivan's work was well known and

Proposed Liberal Club, St George's Place, Glasgow, 1907. *The British Architect,* 1907.

admired by students at the Glasgow School of Art at this time,[10] and Salmon lectured there, he would undoubtedly have been aware of Sullivan's buildings. Once again the scheme could be viewed as an attempt to find a style acceptable to public tastes — as discussed earlier — more significantly, it could also be reflective of an aesthetic exploration being pursued on both sides of the Atlantic.

A return to domestic commissions in Kilmacolm in 1909 allowed Salmon to continue to refine and further develop his ideas on house design. In contrast to the previous jobs, which were carried out for well-to-do professionals, this next scheme was for a speculative cottage development specifically for rent or purchase by those on modest incomes. The project consists of a terrace of six two-storey cottages each provided with the minimum of accommodation and access to communal garden areas. Limited budgets dictated not only the basic provision of space and amenities but also economy and simplicity of construction, materials and detail. The cottages have brick roughcast walls with stone dressings around the openings, half-timbered gables and red tiled roofs. There is no decoration or ornament. Salmon relies for effect solely on the combination of simple forms, colours and textures. This rational design creed of economy was applied for the solution to the firm's final major commercial project: the Lion Chambers, 170-72 Hope Street, Glasgow.

'On every hand the study of architecture encounters physics, statics and dynamics, suggesting, controlling, justifying its design. It is open to us, therefore, to look in buildings for the logical expression of material properties and material laws. Without these, architecture is impossible, its history unintelligible.'

Geoffrey Scott, *The Architecture of Humanism* (1914)

ARCHITECTURAL ANALYSIS:
THE LION CHAMBERS: FROM ART NOUVEAU TO MODERNISM

In 1904 the firm developed a commission to design and build a block of chambers for a corner site at the junction of Hope Street and Bath Lane in Glasgow city centre. The client was William George Black, a Glasgow lawyer and a man of prolific writings and known artistic interests. He was a lay-member of the Glasgow Art Club and it was probably through the Salmons' membership of the same club that the firm gained the commission. Still more so than at St Vincent Street Chambers, the site for these offices was exceptionally small, only 33 feet by 46 feet, yet had to accommodate an extensive office area with adequate day-lighting. It rapidly became apparent that if the accommodation was planned in an economic spatial arrangement, the use of traditional load-bearing construction techniques — with adequate fire protection — would render the room dimensions below that allowable for occupation. Furthermore, as only a three feet strip of Bath Lane could be enclosed to locate ground scaffolding, and Hope Street not at all, the implications of the on-site construction process would also have to be carefully considered at the design stage. The solution to these constraints was to be found in the use of reinforced concrete for the construction, which W. J. Anderson — Salmon's mentor at Leiper's office — had explored in the 1890s, and which by 1904 was being widely reported upon[1] and used in both Europe and America. An early example had in fact been executed in Glasgow at Jessie Street, Polmadie, 1903, which Salmon studied, while several London theatres, including the Garrick and the Royal English Opera House, had also made use of the new technology. His frequent visits to the capital and the Continent, where the two main systems had been developed by Edward Coignet (fl.1850) in France and his competitor François Hennebique (1843-1921) in Belgium, would undoubtedly have raised this awareness further.[2]

To the designers of the early twentieth century the main properties offered by reinforced concrete were its natural resistance to fire and its relatively high load-bearing capacity for small section dimensions and weight. Walls, floors, columns and beams could be reduced to sizes never before possible, and by adjustment of the reinforcing bars any shape of window could be designed. Additionally, because of the floor-by-floor construction process, there was no need to provide supporting ground scaffolding. Salmon and Gillespie realised that the restrictions of

brief, site and legislation affecting the design of the Lion Chambers demanded that reinforced concrete be used. The scheme was developed over a three year period from drawing board to completion, with the firm engaging Louis Gustave Mouchel to design the structural system, and appointing the Hennebique Contracting Company of Leeds to execute the construction work, perhaps one of the earliest management type of building contracts. The resulting design rises 90 feet into the air — 100 feet from the basement — and is built around a structure of 21 columns, each one starting 13 inches square, tapering to eight inches at their summit. The loads from the cantilevered floors are transferred via this column arrangement to a raft foundation at basement level and the forces thereafter distributed equally across the whole site.

During construction advantage was taken of the monolithic nature of the system to cantilever flying scaffolds out from each floor, thus allowing work on the elevations of the building to be executed as necessary, and avoiding the limitations of scaffolding interfering with the congested street life below. Since all the loads from the floors were to be carried by the columns and beams, none of the walls were load-bearing either internally or externally. In consequence the internal walls were light-weight items prefabricated off-site in panels known as 'Mack Partitions', and the outside walls were reduced to a mere four inches thick, thus ensuring compliance of the room sizes with the contemporary legislation. With the walls relieved of any load-bearing function, complete design freedom in the elevational treatment was possible. The west elevation is a virtuoso play on solid and void, being composed of a gable end façade punctuated by square, rectangular, semi-circular, and key-hole shaped windows, all juxtaposed with an octagonal turret running through the building's eight storeys. Although an overall balance prevails, it is somewhat random in its elemental composition, recalling Mackintosh's intuitive touch and perhaps anticipating Kandinsky's observation that the 'haphazard arrangement of forms may be the future of artistic harmony'.[3] The strong vertical emphasis, and the overall compositional balance, recalls the Athenaeum Theatre of more than a decade earlier, but at a detail level they differ significantly. Salmon and Gillespie recognised the innate character of the new mode of construction and made 'no effort ... to imitate a stone or brick building'.[4] There are no richly carved applied features, pediments or balconies on

The Mitchell Library, Cultural and Leisure Services

Published illustration of the Lion Chambers: perspective drawn by John Gaff Gillespie. *Building Industries,* 1906.

RCAHMS

Decorated corbels at fifth floor level, the Lion Chambers.

RCAHMS

Heraldic emblem, the Lion Chambers.

View from the south-west of the Lion Chambers.

RCAHMS

the Lion Chambers, 'the cornices, strings, and other run moulds were formed by timbering and ... the other architectural enrichments such as medallions, keystones and busts ... [were] ... formed by means of strong plaster moulds reinforced with steel',[5] and integrated structurally and formally into the façade.

Interesting traditional features on the street elevation are the roll mouldings at the windows, borrowed from 'The Hatrack' and Northernhay, and a group of mock corbels at the fifth floor level — perhaps borrowed from Anderson's Napier House, Govan Road, 1899. Corbels were historically used to support an overhanging floor, but in this instance the concrete frame supports the loads and the corbels perform no function. Here, Salmon may be playing an architectural joke on the viewer by poking fun at traditional constructional methods. The joke is made all the more obvious by the excessive number and garish carving of the corbels — an effect which Robert Venturi has referred to as 'perspective by incongruity',[6] or the changing of the meaning of an object by altering either its location or scale, *viz* 'old clichés in new settings achieve rich meanings which are ambiguously both old and new, banal and vivid'.[7] This *joie de vivre* is mirrored in the varied shapes and sizes of the windows in a dexterous demonstration of the possibilities offered by the plastic nature of concrete. Because of the thinness of the walls, the windows appear almost flush with the plane of the façade, a setting that makes the elevation appear like a thin sheet without dimension in depth, and endows the building with a remarkable feeling of soaring lightness and volume. These effects are particularly pronounced on the north elevation: this is composed of an extensive rippling glass grid of windows which functionally allows the maximum amount of daylight into the offices, and aesthetically pushes the proportion of void to solid to its limit. It is a direct development from Salmon's rear elevation for the Mercantile Chambers, with the thin spandrel panels and steel windows having been adapted to suit thin-wall concrete construction. The resulting lightness suggests a tightly bound spacious volume, an effect heightened by the gentle modulation of the grid plane.[8]

In 1908 Salmon read a paper to the Glasgow Institute of Architects, titled 'The Decoration of Steel And Reinforced Concrete Structures', which confirmed not only his convictions regarding the appropriate use and treatment of concrete, but also his design approach to the art of architecture. He advocated that aspects of 'the Scottish style, I mean especially that of the old rough-cast castle',[9] could be adapted for reinforced concrete

© R. O'Donnell

The thin-wall glazed and modulated north elevation of the Lion Chambers.

RCAHMS

Castle Fraser, Aberdeenshire.

structures, but was aware of the dangers of falling into the trap of using features that could lead to the building looking like a Scottish castle.[10] Formally, he specifically noted the plain roughcast surfaces, simple corbelling, small cornices, straight lines, and the rarity of arches found in old Scots work. In regard to colour he noted the variations possible in concrete, from light blue-grey to pale buff, but cautioned against using different mixes for one building, observing that 'a design in the spirit of Castle Fraser is independent of a few variations in colour'.[11] Colour contrasts and highlights could, however, be very effectively achieved by incorporating tile work: 'In Spain the effect of domed roofs laid with blue glazed Italian shaped tiles is superb. The blues are by no means uniform, varying in every tile, which adds to the sparkle. In using tiles in reinforced concrete work, I think they should be used only to give points of colour.

You must not start out with the idea that concrete is grey ugly stuff, which must be hidden up, but you must add touches of colour so as to cause the grey to assume a beauty by contrast. Thus, if you used touches of cool deep blue and blue-green tiles, the concrete would appear warmer. And in setting the tiles into the wall they should not touch each other, but the concrete should run through between them, and so weave into the wall'.[12]

While the Lion Chambers incorporates many of these aspects — tiling was originally proposed but not carried out — it retains its integrity and looks like a reinforced concrete building. Salmon clarified his views regarding the adaptation of the Scottish style, commenting that 'artistically, each nation should do as much as

possible to preserve a distinctive character. I don't think that we should copy the work of our Scottish Ancestors, but we should develop our style on our own lines'.[13] His esteem for the architecture of his native land recalls the sympathies of Mackintosh,[14] and it is interesting to note that Salmon regarded contemporary criticism of Mackintosh as totally unwarranted, writing, 'It amuses me, knowing the architect of the School of Art as I do and appreciating his work with constant delight, to find that some people think him an outrageous innovator. Why? I think he shows in this building more reverence and inward feeling for Tradition than all the Scottish Antiquarians added together'.[15] Salmon's concern for the Scottish style was, like Mackintosh, for its feeling and spirit, but not necessarily its forms: 'The only Traditions of Art worth repeating are the Traditions of Nobility of character', he wrote.[16] The problem of the appropriate expression and formal handling of reinforced concrete was in fact universal. On the Continent Mouchel himself advocated the load-bearing

RCAHMS

View from the north-west of the Lion Chambers.

capacity of reinforced concrete as suitable for carrying ornamental stone façades. In America A. O. Elzner's Ingalls Building, Cincinnati, 1902-04, was brick — and marble — clad, and elevated like a steel-framed building rather than the concrete from which it was constructed. Elzner, however, did recognise the dilemma associated with establishing a suitable means of expression and foresaw a time when the elevational concrete would be left unclad to create a rational architecture.[17] As regards the Lion Chambers, it may be said that the firm used concrete as concrete.

Salmon forcefully deplored the error of imitating stone in concrete, noting that 'these imitations are so unsuccessful [and] are designed of course by men who could not successfully imitate a good stone building even in stone ... Things should express their purpose'.[18]

In considering ornament Salmon also emphatically rejected 'Futile Decoration',[19] declaring that 'as an ugly woman, loudly dressed and hung with jewellery, accentuates her want of charm, so does a poorly composed structure call attention to its deficiencies by its embellishments ... study economy ... [and] ... Eliminate the unnecessary excrescences'.[20] He did not, however, reject the use of ornament and decoration out of hand. This misconception has led to the erroneous view that a change in design direction in the firm's work took place and therefore compromise in their design approach; and has resulted in the Lion Chambers being viewed as an oddity when compared to the firm's earlier works, particularly 'The Hatrack'. The source of the misconception may lie in Salmon's own words: 'If this new material, reinforced concrete, could induce us to drop all the ridiculous accretion of absurdities which we plaster on to stone, it will indeed have lifted a weight from a world overladen with "ornaments" and "decorations"'.[21] However, by way of contrast he also noted that 'when the design begins to live as a real thing think of decoration. When your Galatea comes to life you may present her with a few jewels and a little clothing'.[22] In the same paper, when recounting the skills and experiences of his sculptor friend Johan Keller, Salmon described in detail the manner in which ornament and decoration could be physically and constructionally accommodated in concrete. In this respect his views may be linked once again with those of Louis Sullivan. Sullivan's democratic aesthetic recognised the significance and importance of ornament to architecture but in contrast to Ruskin, who held that all ornament was sculptural and *the* fundamental element in the creation of architecture, Salmon and Sullivan believed that ornament was merely a tool of the designer and should never be allowed to over-run a design. The controlling influences of a sound concept and balanced composition were always necessary, and elaborate ornamentation in itself would never be sufficient to produce good architecture. The architect had always to retain control and never lose sight of the architectural objective beneath a myriad of decorations. Whether ornament should be used or not was not the question, the real issue was the appropriate extent, application and integration of it in design.

In 1910 the journal *Ferro Concrete* asserted that 'true ferro concrete is characterised by lightness'[23] and specifically singled out the Lion Chambers as 'one of the most successful attempts in this country to develop an appropriate style' for the material.[24] The effect of 'lightness', or lack of mass, had been a persistent issue for Victorian architects since, in Mackintosh's words, 'the advent of the Crystal Palace and the many rosetinted hallucinations of that period'.[25] Mackintosh did not accept a style of architecture without 'stability' or strength. He specifically cautioned against the use of modern materials that have a want of mass or bulk observing that 'iron is much stronger than stone & so a thin clothes pole of metal is as strong as a much bulkier piece of stone or brick but the eye is distressed'.[26] For Mackintosh this negative psychological effect should be avoided at all costs, because 'apart … from any defect in stability or actual comfort the want of appearance of stability is fatal … for either domestic, civil, or ecclesiastical buildings'.[27]

These concerns were not shared by Salmon, who saw in concrete and steel new materials that could release the mind and imagination and reveal new levels and avenues of expression. The truth is that Salmon and Gillespie made no attempt 'to develop an appropriate style' for the use of concrete. By 'getting down to the bedrock of absolute economy'[28] and designing the Lion Chambers 'in a way suited to the nature of the materials … not ashamed of their methods of construction',[29] indeed exploiting the physical properties of concrete and glass 'and in the accentuation of [the] construction',[30] the light and spacious qualities of the design naturally evolved. The building is a direct result of their rational, functional and economic approach to design through which the materials are honestly expressed and the decorative details are formed as an integral part of the construction, creating effect by contrast. This same rationale had in fact been applied to the design of 'The Hatrack'. It was composed, structured and constructed to meet the functional restrictions of site and use, with the decorative carved features not added onto the building, but emerging naturally from the surface to give relief, interest, life and expression. Neither building was the result of a fancy or whim of style on the part of its designer. Both were direct results of the emerging technology and structural learning of the time. As the steel structure for 'The Hatrack' moved to the interior of the building to free the envelope from a load bearing function and allow as much light as possible to influx its depths; so too had the concrete structure of the Lion Chambers. The approach to the design of both is consistent: the differences between the two are their materials of construction, and the appropriate exploitation of

British Architectural Library, RIBA, London

The Ingalls Building, Fourth Street-Vine Street, Cincinnati, Ohio, built 1902-04, by A. O. Elzner. *The Architectural Record,* 1904.

these materials to achieve their full inherent potential of expression. This led to a natural progression from the turning and twisting plastic Art Nouveau of 'The Hatrack', to the light, soaring, Modernism of the Lion Chambers.[31]

The completion of the Lion Chambers turned out to be the last major work carried out by Salmon and Gillespie together in

Glasgow, and they never received the opportunity to develop the stylistic opportunities afforded by reinforced concrete further. The firm did win the competition for the Stirling Municipal Buildings in 1908 with a design by Gillespie which was to be partly constructed using reinforced concrete, but the style was Scots Renaissance, with 'subtle *fin-de-siècle* nuances in the detailing'.[32]

In 1909 Gillespie won another competition, this time for a ferro-concrete shop design which was considered 'best for the specific material, [being] an articulation of mass as opposed to the usual constructive details of stone or brick'.[33] The design reveals a development towards Art Deco in its use of chevron forms and rectangular black framing at the stepped gable, which also anticipates details of Josef Hoffmann's Palais Stocklet, Brussels, 1910. Unfortunately there was never any intention that it should be built. (See Addendum)

The Lion Chambers is rightly recognised as one of the pioneering works of the Modern Movement and may be viewed as the tangible representation of Salmon's design philosophy stated as follows:

'Don't for the sake of heaven and earth think for a moment of being artistic, or you are lost. Be sane and sensible; ignore all teaching and everything that anyone has ever said about art or style, and be only practical and all these things shall be added unto you ... beauty is the absence of ugliness ... How magnificent are the works of those engineers who have avoided "architecture" ... [as] ... "Beauty unadorned is adorned the most"'.[34]

How closely this statement anticipates Mies van der Rohe's aphorism that 'Less is More'.

·You ask how are you to judge architecture,
just as you judge painting or sculpture —
form, colour, proportion all visible qualities —
and the one great invisable [sic] quality in all art, soul.'

Charles Rennie Mackintosh, *Architecture* (1893)

'The artist must have something to say, for mastery over form is not
his goal, but rather the adapting of form to its inner meaning.'

Wassily Kandinsky, *Concerning the Spiritual in Art* (1914)

CONCLUSION

James Salmon, like his friend Charles Rennie Mackintosh, stands out among his Scottish contemporaries on the basis of a relatively small number of designs which were strikingly original and adventurous, reflecting a man of original thought who approached all problems encountered in design and life with complete openness of mind. Among recent commentators, Professor David Walker has acclaimed Salmon as a master of Art Nouveau, Gavin Stamp rated him a major European talent, and Alistair Service has ranked his buildings as 'comparable in individuality',[1] with those of Mackintosh. In their own lifetimes Salmon and Gillespie drew critical acclaim at home and abroad, being favourably reviewed in British, French and German periodicals, and exhibited in Turin and Belgrade. *The Studio* magazine was moved to comment that:

'The charm of the work of these architects is not due to the prevailing use of any particular materials, nor is to be found in any abject reverence for precedent, nor in adherence to any given style, though at the same time it cannot be said that the originality of thought and treatment is that of eccentricity masquerading under a nobler name. Knowledge of the architecture of the past is kept in its rightly subordinate place by equally full recognition of the modified conditions of the present, and the result is sane and practical'.[2]

Even that most incisive of critics Horace Townsend — brother of the renowned English architect Charles Harrison Townsend — commended their work. But in our own day, like all other Glasgow Style designers, Salmon and Gillespie have been overshadowed by the torrent of publishing on Mackintosh, and this phenomenon has made comparisons between them both unavoidable and peculiarly difficult. While Mackintosh is justly regarded as the most individual exponent of the Glasgow Style, who led and influenced his contemporaries by the sheer originality and force of his talent, he did not work in a cultural vacuum and his friendship with Salmon and Gillespie was certainly no one-way exchange of formal references. They were too honest and too original to have to plagiarise and for all Mackintosh's uniqueness it is difficult to overlook the formal similarities between later work of his and some of the earlier work of Salmon and Gillespie. Perhaps the canted bays on the south elevation of the Temperance League Offices, 1893, and the rear elevation of the Mercantile Chambers, 1896-98, found an echo in Mackintosh's *Daily Record* Office, 1900; while the Art Nouveau curves and lines of the copper relief panels at 79 West Regent Street, 1900-04, seem closely related to

© R. O'Donnell

Stone motif detail to rear elevation of Scotland Street School, 1904-06, by C. R. Mackintosh.

Copper panel with stylised Coat-of-Arms of Glasgow, 79 West Regent Street by Salmon, 1900-04.

RCAHMS

A sweeping ogee moulding used in combination with block and circle forms all 'crowned' by a fluid Art Nouveau lamp, at the entrance to Rowantreehill.

East elevation of the Glasgow School of Art, built 1897-99, by C. R. Mackintosh.

the stone relief motifs on the rear elevation of Mackintosh's Scotland Street School, 1904-06. The severe extended eaves at Govan Cross Savings Bank, 1897, and Salmon's lively ogee lintel with juxtaposed squares and circles over the entrance to Rowantreehill, 1898, may have been reinterpreted by Mackintosh on the north and east elevations of the Art School respectively.[3] In terms of raw functionalism Salmon and Mackintosh met on common ground, relying on the starkness of the gridded window: Salmon for the Lion Chambers, 1904-07; and Mackintosh for the

west elevation of the Art School, 1907-09. Both works display a soaring purity, rooted in the clarity of their detailing.

However, one also finds traces of Mackintosh in Salmon. The extended cornice lines of the capitals at the St Vincent Chambers, 1898-99, appear related in treatment to the cornices of the tower at Queen's Cross Church 1897-99, and of the second floor turret window on the Art School's east elevation. The ogee turret and exposed eaves overhang of the *Glasgow Herald* building, 1893-95, and the oriental curved eaves overhang of the Martyrs' Public School, 1895-96, both predate the capping and extended eaves

Detail of the grid pattern to the north elevation of the Lion Chambers, built 1904-07.

treatment of St Vincent Street Chambers. That both Salmon and Mackintosh were influenced by Celtic philosophy has already been discussed, but at a formal level an interesting similarity exists between Mackintosh's watercolour *The Tree of Personal Effort* of 1895 and Salmon's hall screen design for the Glasgow Exhibition of 1901. If one considers the framing arch of the screen as mirroring that of the sun in the watercolour, then the screen columns equate to the tree forms of the painting, splitting into branches at the arch and ultimately blossoming into framing voids around the carved figures — just as Mackintosh's trees bud and bloom.[4] The formal relationship is repeated in the firm's electric clock design for the same exhibition, in which branching tree forms front the hearth opening, and the line tracery of the mid section grows organically upwards. Aside from the work of Mackintosh, David Walker has identified the influence of the Mercantile Chambers' rear elevation of canted bay windows on the work of Burnet and Campbell: particularly at the Atlantic

Gridded bay windows to the west elevation of the Glasgow School of Art, built 1907-09.

The sweeping cornice and extended pilaster capital detail to the window openings of the St Vincent Chambers.

Elongated cornice to Queen's Cross Church, 1897-99, by C. R. Mackintosh.

Chambers, 1899, and the Edinburgh Life Assurance offices, 1906. He has also noted a relationship between the upper arcade of the Mercantile Chambers on both that of 157-67 Hope Street, completed by Campbell some six years later in 1902, and the detailing on the Norwich Union office of John Hutchison and T. Ramsay at 125-27 St Vincent Street, 1898. Similarities are also evident between 'The Hatrack' and a tenement block by Salmon's friend Henry Edward Clifford at Bank Street — off University Avenue — Glasgow, 1901. Both have centrally recessed planes flanked by bay windows running the full height to eaves level, extended pilasters, ogee pediments, and corbelling details below projecting upper levels. Although Clifford's building has quite a broad frontage — over 80 foot long — compositionally, both have

an overall vertical emphasis, and terminate with ogee lead cappings and a flurry of scroll and curve forms. While these examples do not provide conclusive evidence of the greater influence of one designer over another, they do illustrate the common forms and details that Salmon, Gillespie, Mackintosh and their contemporaries explored, shared and, perhaps, exchanged.

Both at the time and since, Salmon's reputation was dealt a severe blow through comments made by the widely read German critic, Hermann Muthesius, in his book *Das Englische Haus* (1904). While Muthesius commended the firm's 'broad surfaces, strong rhythms, neutral colour [and] mystical air',[5] he considered that in their exteriors they were 'merely on the lookout for originality ... [following] ... a local style',[6] created by Mackintosh.[7]

For his comments to have any critical validity it would have to be confirmed that Salmon was striving to design to the same conceptual and formal creeds as Mackintosh. This has never been established and would be disputed by modern day Mackintosh authors including David Brett and Alan Crawford, and by the present author. Two of the most thoughtful recent commentators on Mackintosh — Brett, in *C. R. Mackintosh: The Poetics of Workmanship* (1992), and Crawford, in *Charles Rennie Mackintosh* (1995) — have compared his work with Salmon's, and noted that although the character of their detail was generally similar — and they shared an interest in the integration of detail with structure — their principles of elevational composition remained fundamentally different throughout their careers: whether working as Art Nouveau designers or modernists. That Salmon and Mackintosh were both Glasgow Stylists is evident from the common treatment of forms to be found in their work. But the Glasgow Stylists did not form a movement with an absolute ethos and the expression of the work of individual designers could be significantly different, ranging from the fairytale visions of Jessie King, to the stylised romantic imagery of George Walton. Neither Salmon nor Gillespie ever copied Mackintosh's figurative symbolism, or his plain white surfaces and chequered motifs. Their emphasis on the characteristic qualities of different types of timber and stone, and their use of sombre dark colours gave a haunting and mysterious air to their work when compared with the light and subliminal quality of Mackintosh's. They never suppressed timberwork under white paint as Mackintosh did to focus the viewer's attention on the pure sculptural forms of his furniture designs; they always allowed their materials to be seen for what they were, and the depth and richness of the lustre and grain, indeed the spirit within the materials, to be read *with* the forms. They were clearly working to different design agendas.

In considering Salmon and Mackintosh, a comparison may be drawn if one considers the work of Picasso and Braque of the 1910s. They both painted in the same place, at the same time, within the same style, but each other's work is equally distinct. Perhaps where Picasso's creativeness was born of natural genius and Braque's was the offspring of meditation, so it was also with Mackintosh and Salmon. While Mackintosh designed intuitively, operating at a formal level led by his soul, Salmon designed analytically led by the tectonic rationale of his mind. In accepting that Braque's paintings are no less masterpieces than Picasso's, one should also accept that Salmon's buildings are no less

Tree of Personal Effort, 1895, C. R. Mackintosh. Note the compositional similarity with Salmon's later hallway screen design of 1901.

masterpieces than Mackintosh's. Muthesius was in fact fundamentally wrong in his assessment of Salmon, because in gauging his work against that of Mackintosh he was not comparing like with like: perhaps the cruelest twist of fate is that Muthesius made his observations in 1898, did not publish them until 1904, and in fact never saw the main corpus of Salmon's work. Furthermore, Muthesius did not discuss the firm's banks or chambers at all.

While Salmon used Art Nouveau forms during the early part of his career, it is too simplistic to categorise him as an Art Nouveau architect who later rebelled against the use of such forms because of a change in his design approach. Brett has noted that a gradual rationalisation occurred in the work of designers of the period

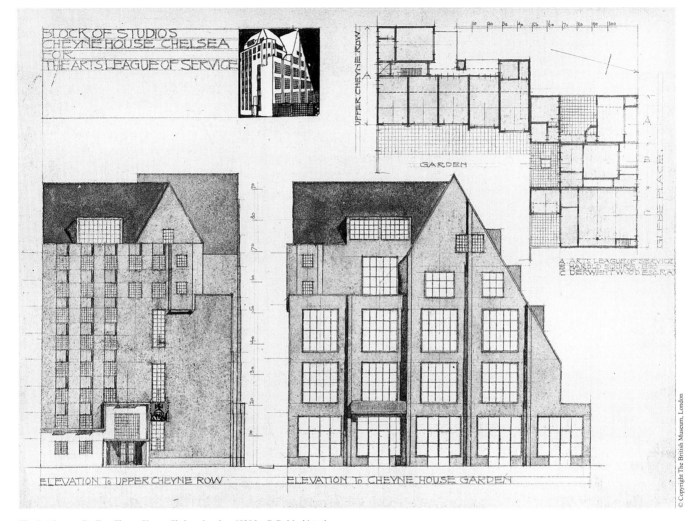

The Arts League Studios, Cheyne House, Chelsea, London, 1920 by C. R. Mackintosh.

generally, including Mackintosh, reflecting a developing trend away from the ornate and organic towards the austere and rectilinear. While Salmon was clearly sympathetic to this trend, his work and that of his contemporaries also has to be considered in the context of the developing technology of the time. In designs such as the Mercantile Chambers, the alterations to the offices at 79 West Regent Street, and the interiors at 22 Park Circus, the

sinuous Art Nouveau forms and rhythms are obvious. Equally obvious, however, is the close control exercised over their use: the decoration always plays a rôle subordinate to the overall tectonic concept, a discipline recognised by *The Builder* in regard to the Mercantile Chambers and admirably demonstrated by St Vincent Street Chambers. The rippling effect of 'The Hatrack' was achieved through a successful marriage between modern structural

Corner detail of the gable-end façade juxtaposed against the part detached corner turret, Lion Chambers.

developments in steel and contemporary sculptural techniques in the treatment of stone. But while the building's expression is dependent on the skill of the sculptor, the overall impact of the design is tectonic. As the new technology progressed into reinforced concrete Salmon reduced the level of decoration, responding not simply to the spirit of the age, but more particularly to the question of the continuing relevancy of ornament being posed by the new material — and ultimately by the advent of mass production and the machine aesthetic. The Lion Chambers in turn does not depend on the skill of the sculptor for effect, and consequently the expression itself is different. The rational exploitation of the structural concrete system allowed the creation of an extensive area of modulated glazing which emphasised the depth and volume of the contained space. Perhaps

more than any other of his works, these two buildings most closely follow Salmon's architectural creed and express his belief in a cosmos of eternal change. The former achieves it in mass terms where the living solid (the stone) is striving to escape from the suffocating void (the glass). The impact being heightened by the stress between the solid slender wrought framework and the mysterious planes of glass void, the character of the relationship being subtly influenced by the play of light and dark reflections through the day. In Lion Chambers, the tension is created between the binding glazed grid and broad expanse of white elevations — the modest depth of which is emphasised by the flush windows — and the internal volume itself, here representing the living spirit, that seems almost to physically push the concrete and glass out to their very limits.[8] Both designs are a complete expression of a philosophical attitude, determined both by the circumstances prevalent and the resources available at a moment in time.

The Lion Chambers also presents an interesting historical turning-point when considering the work and writings of Salmon's contemporaries. Burnet and Campbell pursued a modern idiom with Edwardian Baroque details, developing a high style culminating in the verticality, mass, and strength of the McGeoch Ironmongery Store, West Campbell Street, Glasgow, 1905-10 (demolished), and the Northern Insurance Building, St Vincent Street, Glasgow, 1908. These buildings recall Mackintosh's statement of 1892, 'Stability ... Strength itself will be a criterion of the excellency of the architecture ... So much is Architecture dependent on this that it requires not only the real fact but the appearance and will prefer of two equally substantial materials the one which has most bulk I think that you will admit that it is the want of apparent strength which is the chief blemish of modern street Architecture'.[9] In considering modern materials Mackintosh was again specific commenting that 'iron and glass though eminently suitable for many purposes will never worthily take the place of stone because of this defect the want of mass'.[10] These words confirm Mackintosh's concern for aesthetic precedent over technological opportunity. The volume and lightness of the Lion Chambers, especially at the northern elevation, flies in the face of such traditionalism, and anticipates the glass, concrete and steel office blocks of the inter-war years. Prior to Brett, Howarth identifed a rationalisation process in Mackintosh's later work which he felt anticipated the plastic expression possible in concrete construction, but he additionally felt Mackintosh failed to rise to the opportunity presented by the Arts League Studios of

1920. While he noted a romantic exploration of forms in the Glebe Place façade of the individual studio houses, he dismissed the elevations to Cheyne House Garden, Upper Cheyne Row, and the studio block itself, despite Mackintosh considering the latter important enough to be worthy of a perspective illustration.[11] While the studio block was proposed to be constructed of reinforced concrete, and there was an extensive area of glazing designed for the garden side elevation, Crawford observed that the designs 'height and mass brought Scotland' to mind,[12] specifically old Scots, in its styling. Additionally, however, there are direct compositional similarities with the Lion Chambers, particularly the balancing of the gable end façade juxtaposed with a part detached octagonal turret. But unlike the Lion Chambers, the proposed wall construction of the studio block was not reduced to a thin plane and any effect of weightlessness would have been reduced, perhaps deliberately so, given Mackintosh's demand for architectural stability and mass. The significant issue raised by the design is that in 1920 Mackintosh appears to have been exploring harmonies and aesthetic juxtapositions in an abstract sculptural balance of concrete masses and blocks. Salmon by contrast had seized the opportunity presented 15 years earlier to focus on the treatment of a constrained volume bound by concrete and glass. It may be that Mackintosh's approach is linked to his focus and instinct for aesthetic form, while Salmon's may be traced to his rationale of analysis, function and economy.

Salmon's development from the sinuous, restless Art Nouveau forms of the pre-1900 designs to Modernism and the emphasis on basic geometries, plain surfaces and the reduction of decoration in the post-1900 work, contains within it his real contribution to architecture. Along with Gillespie his designs were always developing and experimenting with motif, composition, structure and construction. They were in a constant state of flux, never repeating that which had gone before, never at rest, always developing and preparing for that which was to come. Although his imagination remained undiminished, it is a tragedy that following the Lion Chambers Salmon never got an opportunity to develop his ideas in concrete construction further.

Always looking towards the architecture of the future, Salmon declared: 'One method which I have not seen done, but which would be most interesting to work out, is to use nothing but steel for the supports, walls, and windows, building the walls as a steel ship is built, making use of the lines of rivets and joints of plates ... If not steel, then copper or lead ... There are also those composition metals to be had — thin steel plates with thin surfaces of brass or aluminium'.[13]

In this statement alone Salmon leaves his contemporaries far behind, anticipating — theoretically at least — the ship aesthetic of the International Style, the technological imagination of Buckminster Fuller and the spiritual purity of Mies van der Rohe.

'To copy old buildings is to re-write a tale that is already written. To take a bit from here and a bit from there is only to plagiarise from more sources than one ... You must study the ancient buildings to learn the science of building and also to read the meanings which they tell us. But while you must do this you have your own story to tell. Tell it in your own words and in your own way'.[14]

'The great point for architects is to have great ideas, to ignore the prejudices of the brief time in which we happen to live, and to design and build for eternity according to our lights'.[15]

James Salmon
1873-1924

ADDENDUM: GILLESPIE, KIDD & COIA

Following the dissolution of the partnership, Gillespie continued to practice from the Mercantile Chambers. The split with Salmon was reported to have been amicable and the available evidence confirms this view. Apart from Salmon's support for Gillespie and Kidd in their applications to join the Incorporation of Architects in Scotland [previously noted], there is also a friendly and humorous exchange between them recorded in the practice's Letterbooks, involving the borrowing of a dumpy level — and its non-timeous return to Salmon!

In 1915 Gillespie took on Jack Coia — who had just graduated, with much distinction, from the Glasgow School of Art — as an assistant;[1] and in 1918, after 20 years' faithful service, made William Alexander Kidd his partner. Much of the firm's work during the war and the lean years that followed is not particularly memorable, although it remained varied. Projects included golf clubhouses at Pollok and Gourock — both won in competition — tenement work in Stirling, alterations to J. & B. Stevensons bakeries in Glasgow, and a continuing design remit for the British Linen Company Bank. The outstanding project they completed over the war years was the Stirling Municipal Buildings complex, which proved to be not only a valuable commission financially, but also benefited the office profile, attracting very favourable reviews. The design borrowed elements from Falkland and Holyrood palaces, and re-interpreted them in a modern idiom. Of particular note were the boldly handled paired stair-tower forms, which recalled Mackintosh at Scotland Street School. Gillespie also revived his links with Albert Hodge through this project commissioning medallion work from him, which also reconfirmed his own sculptural preferences.

By the 1920s the practice had broadened its client base. It became involved in the design and fitting out of ship interiors, executing those of the *S.S. Curraghmore* and *S.S. Kennedine* for the ship-building firm Messrs William Denny of Greenock.[2]

The most stylistically interesting design of this later period was for offices at 118 Union Street, Glasgow (demolished), adjoining the Ca'd'Oro building of John Honeyman. Gillespie produced the initial sketches allowing his young protégé Coia to develop the working drawings; but sadly before work reached a conclusion, and following a short period of illness, Gillespie died on 7 May 1926.[3] Kidd duly made Coia his partner and allowed him to continue the project's development, but tragically he also died

Stirling Municipal Buildings, Corn Exchange-King Street, Stirling, by John Gaff Gillespie. Executed between 1915-18, it was never fully completed to Gillespie's winning scheme of 1908.

before it was finished — in 1929 — leaving Coia to complete the work on his own.

The Union Street offices reinterpreted the articulation and massing of Gillespie's ferro-concrete shop design of 1909 — once again utilising the Hennebique reinforced concrete system under the supervision of L. G. Mouchel as engineer — and its distinctive detailing of chevrons, chequered mouldings and tile framing.[4] But the style was American Art Deco rather than modernist, perhaps reflecting Gillespie's awareness of developments across the Atlantic through his subscription in the

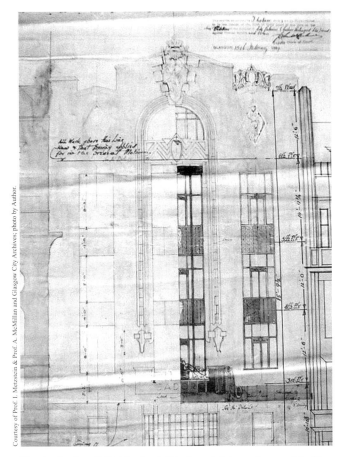

Elevation drawing of 118 Union Street. Note the central chevron forms, and the thin metal frame and panel construction proposed to the bays.

early 1920s to the New York-based periodical, *American Architect*.

Demolished during the 1980s despite local protest, the building tantalisingly hinted at Gillespie's view of the future treatment of reinforced concrete. It also provided the young Coia, a future RIBA Gold Medal winner, with a springing-point from which to continue and develop the legacy of his master's architectural vision.

Gillespie's Art Deco influenced competition winning entry for a Ferro-Concrete, Shop Design, 1909. *The British Architect,* 1909.

NOTES

BACKGROUND:
THE SECOND CITY AND ARCHITECTURE

1. Oakley, C. A., *The Second City*, Blackie & Son Ltd, 3rd edition, 1976, p. 148.
2. The art establishments in Edinburgh and London initially coolly received the paintings of the Glasgow Boys. However, abroad, John Lavery, James Paterson and Alexander Roche were all favourably received, particularly at the Munich Exhibition of 1890, and the Paris Salons. Significantly, along with contemporaries including William McTaggart, George Henry, and John Quinton Pringle, their paintings are now sought worldwide.
3. In time the steel frame itself became more positively expressed and the elevational emphasis gradually more vertical, ultimately becoming a gridded veneer with the advent of reinforced concrete construction.
4. Burnet could have seen their work during a visit to America in 1896.
5. Goodhart-Rendel, H. S., quoted in Stamp, G., 'Mackintosh, Burnet and Modernity', in *Architectural Heritage III - The Journal of the Architectural Heritage Society of Scotland: The Age of Mackintosh*, Edinburgh University Press, 1992, p. 9.
6. Stamp, G., *op. cit.*, p. 9.
7. This Celtic symbolism and imagery also inspired a later stunning stained glass window by Gauld for Rosehaugh House, 1896. The pagan druid tribe's reverence for the natural world and their cult of the personification of trees focusing on the *Craobh an Elois*, or Tree of Knowledge, later became a recurring theme in the watercolours of Mackintosh, MacNair, and the Macdonald sisters Margaret and Frances.
8. John Duncan was a leading figure in the 'Celtic Revival' and shared a studio with George Dutch Davidson. Duncan's *Riders of the Sidhe*, 1911, and Davidson's *The Hills of Dream*, 1899, both in Dundee City Art Gallery, illustrate the importance of Celtic mythology to Scottish art of this period.
9. The Art Nouveau style flourished in Continental Europe and Britain at the turn of the century, the term embracing *Jugendstil* ('Youth Style'), *Secessionstil* ('Secession Style'), Liberty Style, Modern Style, and Glasgow Style in different countries. It derived its name from a specialist Japanese art shop opened in 1885 by Samuel Bing, a native of Hamburg living in Paris. As well as oriental *objets d'art* Bing promoted the growing popular interest in the decorative arts, exhibiting the work of Bonnard, Toulouse-Lautrec, Van de Velde, Rodin, Carrière, Gallé, Tiffany, Bearsdley and Scotland's own Charles Rennie Mackintosh.
10. Crane, W., in Waddel, R., *The Art Nouveau Style*, Dover Publications Inc., 1977, p. x.
11. Van de Velde, H., in Waddel, R., *op. cit.*
12. Grasset, E., in Waddel, R., *op. cit.*
13. In various areas of Scotland other architects were developing their own interpretations of this northern Art Nouveau, such as W. D. McLennan in Paisley and W. G. Lamond in Dundee.

BIOGRAPHY:
PRE 1888: JAMES SALMON SENIOR AND WILLIAM FORREST SALMON

1. RIBA fellowship nomination papers, 20 October1876.
2. Gomme, A. and Walker, D., *The Architecture of Glasgow*, Lund Humphries, London, 2nd edition, 1987, p. 297.
3. James Salmon senior wrote a pastoral comedy called *Gowandean* which was illustrated by Sir Daniel Macnee RSA the nationally renowned portrait artist.
4. The Glasgow Architectural Society was not exclusive to architects but also invited guest speakers including the sculptor JohnMossman (1817-1890), the stained glass designer Daniel Cottier (1838-1891) and the artisan timber carver John Crawford (*fl.*1873-1910).
5. *The Bailie*, 30 October 1872, No. 2.
6. *The Bailie*, 30 October 1872, No. 2.
7. In Walker, D., *The Scottish Art Review*, Vol. X, no. 3, p. 18.
8. Smith's architectural achievements have been largely over-shadowed by the scandal surrounding his daughter Madeleine, who was at the centre of one of the most controversial murder cases in Scottish history.
9. See Savage, P., *Lorimer and the Edinburgh Craft Designers*, Paul Harris Publishing, 1980; Walker, D. W., 'The Salmon Collection', unpublished RCAHMS catalogue, p. 4. Donnelly, M., *Glasgow Stained Glass*, Glasgow Museums and Art Galleries, p. 11 notes that James Moyr Smith was at Salmon & Son about this time.
10. It is possible that William Forrest (and Scott Morton) may have met with Moyr Smith in London, between Moyr Smith's arrival in 1864 and Salmon's departure in 1866.
11. *RIBA Journal*, 11 November 1911, Vol. 19, p. 27.
12. Helen Russel Salmon was a founder member of the Glasgow Society of Lady Artists. Two of G. G. Anderson's cartoons survive within the Salmon Collection, RCAHMS.
13. *RIBA Journal*, 11 November 1911, Vol. 19, p. 27.
14. William Forrest Salmon's obituary in the *RIBA Journal*, 11 November 1911, Vol. 19, p. 27, notes 'He used every effort towards raising the status of the staff and the high place which this school now has in this respect is largely due to his constant endeavours.'
15. Salmon, W. F., 'The Master Wright and The Architect', in *The Glasgow Advertiser and Property Circular*, 19 December 1893.
16. *Ibid.*
17. *Ibid.*
18. *Ibid.*
19. Donnelly, M., *Glasgow Stained Glass*, Glasgow Museum and Art Galleries, 1981, p. 20. William exhibited his own watercolours and photographs of Gallowhill at the Glasgow Institute of Fine Art exhibitions during the 1890s.
20. David Valentine Wylie (1857-1930) also trained with James and William.
21. Ritchie went on to design St Bride's Church, West Kilbride, 1881.
22. William Forrest had also assisted in the drawing work for Glasgow University, 1866-71, although Alexander Thomson dismissed the new buildings as 'sixteenth century Scottish architecture clothed in fourteenth century French details' — from Gomme, A., and Walker, D., *op. cit.* p. 169.
23. William was also chosen as the Glasgow Institute of Architects representative to Glasgow District Council (*Building Industries*, 15 April 1896); and was latterly called upon to act as an arbiter in contractual disputes (*Building Industries*, 16 January 1906).
24. 'Aunt Mina', as she was affectionately known, had looked after their grandfather's household after the death of her own mother in 1881 and remained close to the boys throughout their lives.

BIOGRAPHY:

1888-1895: YOUTH AND TRAINING

1. Mackintosh, C. R., in Robertson, P., *Charles Rennie Mackintosh: the Architectural Papers*, University of Glasgow and White Cockade Publishing, 1990, p. 208. Newbery's ideas, associations and contacts would have attracted William Forrest's sympathies with Arts and Crafts issues.
2. *Glasgow School of Art Prospectus*, 1900-01, p. 8.
3. His tutors at the Art School included not only his father but also William Leiper, John James Burnet, John Archibald Campbell, and John Keppie.
4. *RIBA Journal*, 26 August 1916, p. 302.
5. RIBA Fellowship application papers of William Leiper, 17 March 1881.
6. Leiper bequeathed a painting of his mother by McTaggart to the RSA.
7. See Gomme, A. and Walker, D., *Architecture of Glasgow*, and W. J. Anderson's nomination papers to the RIBA.
8. *Building Industries*, 16 May 1900.
9. *RIBA Journal*, 28 April 1900, p. 312.
10. *Ibid*. p. 313.
11. Anderson published his first book *Architectural Studies In Italy* in 1890 and set up on his own account a year later. Following a fatal accident during the construction of Napier House he had to receive treatment for depression and although entirely blameless for the incident, he tragically committed suicide in 1900.
12. William Hunter McNab was Leiper's assistant and held him in high regard.
13. *RIBA Journal*, 26 August 1916, p. 304.
14. See Dean of Guild drawing submissions between March 1895 and April 1895. The former were submitted under the title 'W. F. Salmon', the latter under the title 'J. Salmon & Son'. After James left for Leiper's office in 1890, William Forrest Salmon used his own name for the firm - dropping "James Salmon & Son". When he returned in 1895, Forrest Salmon restored the practice's original title.
15. Salmon, W. F., 'The Master Wright and the Architect', in *Glasgow Advertiser and Property Circular*, 19 December 1893.
16. William has been dismissed as 'the commercial traveler of the firm rather than an architect', and reported as latterly 'never seen with a pencil in his hand' — from Gomme, A. and Walker, D., *op. cit.* p. 222. Although these comments may indeed apply to his later years they ignore his recorded artistic talents, his commendable design work at Gallowhill, and his development, contribution and support for the crafts and educational philosophy which Newbery was pursuing in Glasgow.

BIOGRAPHY:

1895-1913: RISE AND FALL

1. The different qualities of the two are also evident in the character of their work, when comparing Salmon's flamboyant 'Hatrack' with Gillespie's restrained Govan Cross Bank, or the ornate 22 Park Circus by Salmon with the severe 12 University Gardens by Gillespie.
2. James viewed the architect's life as one of continuous education; this in advance of today's Continuing Professional Development requirements. His insistence on engaging in life's activities may be viewed as an extension of the Arts and Crafts belief that intimate experience and working knowledge are the keys to understanding the many dimensions of any craft; in Salmon's case architecture.
3. Salmon, J., 'Architects - Their Relaxation', in *The Architect's and Builder's Journal*, 9 December 1896 (text of paper read to the Glasgow Architectural Association, 1 December 1896).
4. *Ibid.*
5. *Ibid.*
6. *Ibid.* See also Walker, A., letter to the *Glasgow Herald*, 21.3.1987- interviewed by author.
7. Jack Coia (1898-1981) recounted that 'both [Salmon and Gillespie] were great friends of Mackintosh, at one time the three were regular drinking friends!' - from Coia's draft for his RIBA Gold Medal speech, held by RIAS. It is also worth noting the Salmons and the Mackintoshes and their circle, all enjoyed frequent social evenings with the Newberys (author's interview with Mary Newbery Sturrock, March 1982).
8. Text dated 1903 held in the Salmon Collection at RCAHMS.
9. *The Bailie*, 6 January 1909, p. 1.
10. He rose to become House Surgeon at the Royal Infirmary and later became Assistant Medical Officer at the City Poorhouse (*The Bailie*, 6 January 1909). Salmon's friendship with Devon would increase his awareness of the health and social problems facing Glasgow's poor.

11. *The Scottish Architect*, March 1909.
12. *Garden Cities and Town Planning*, December 1909, p. 185. Separate references have recently emerged to a 'New Village' scheme designed in 1902-03 by the firm for Woodilee Hospital (Walker, D. W., 'The Salmon Collection', unpublished RCAHMS catalogue, p. 11); and the execution of ten workmens cottages, for the Steel Company of Scotland, 1907-8.
13. *Vista* (the magazine of the Glasgow School of Architecture Club), 1908-10, p. 44.
14. This difference in style between the work of the two is discussed in detail later.

BIOGRAPHY:

1913-1924: FINAL YEARS

1. *The Times*, 6 October 1902.
2. Oakley, C. A. *op. cit.* p. 200.
3. Author's interview with Mary Newbery Sturrock, March 1982.
4. Christmas card to Salmon from J. M. K. Taylor, 16 Rue de La Grand Chaumiere, Paris 6, dated 1915, originally held in collection of David Miller.
5. Arranged along the same style and economic lines of earlier co-partnership cottages in Kilmacolm (1909).
6. One hut built in association with the YMCA on the island of Flotta in the Orkneys cost £6,954 19s. Built in 1917, the excessive cost of the building was a result of the 'wild conditions, the workmen being cut off from supplies during weeks of storm, and reduced to half and quarter rations. Water had to be bored for, hundreds of feet down into the Old Red Sandstone. This rock was also quarried from the cliffs on the shore, and hauled up by an oil engine to build the necessarily stout walls' (*The Bailie*, 23 January 1918, p. 1).
7. *The Bailie*, 23 January 1918, p. 1.
8. Details held in the Salmon Collection, RCAHMS. Salmon persistently utilised the geometry of the octagon but it is not yet clear why.
9. *The Bailie*, 23 January 1918, p. 1.
10. *Ibid.*
11. Salmon, J., 'The Art of Building - The Future Evolution of Architecture', in *The Scottish Architect*, March 1909, p. 264.
12. Extract from a letter to *Building Industries*, 16 November 1916.
13. See his article on housing titled 'Mousetraps', in *The Quarterly*, Summer 1922, No. 2.

14. Witnesses of the civil ceremony were Alexander Yuille, a dispensing chemist, and Eileen Brown Orr, Dr Picken's medical partner, and sister of the artist brothers, Stewart, Jack and Munro Orr, whom Salmon came to count among his dearest friends. The Salmons, the Devons, the Orrs and their friends shared many sociable and musical evenings during the following years. At such occasions Salmon would recite his own humorous verses such as 'To-morrow' for the company's entertainment (text preserved in the Salmon Collection, RCAHMS.)

15. It would appear that the fund-raising may have been successful as some work was carried out on the villa, but the precise extent and timing is not certain. On one of his visits to Dubrovnik, Salmon surveyed the villa and was recommended as the architect to carry out alterations to improve its suitability for use as a hospital — but this may only have been done on a good-will basis.

16. See 'In The Balkans', *The Bailie*, 26 January 1921 — 'Mr Salmon was entertained to dinner by the members of the club and subsequently related his experiences. As was to be expected from a humourist like Mr Salmon the lecture was amusing and had many entertaining touches.' See also *Glasgow Herald*, 22 December 1921. Five original texts are preserved within the Salmon Collection, RCAHMS.

17. The Institute's minute books also reveal he remained on sufficiently amicable terms with Gillespie to propose both him and William Alexander Kidd (Gillespie's junior partner) for membership. See also Addendum: Gillespie, Kidd & Coia.

18. Salmon, J., 'American Architecture' in *The Quarterly*, Summer 1922, no. 2, p. 17.

19. *Ibid.*

20. Submissions by other Glasgow architects Hutton & Taylor and A. Hamilton Scott & J. A. W. Grant received commendations.

21. Devon, J., 'James Salmon — An Appreciation', *Glasgow Herald*, 5 May 1924, ref. 7f.

22. Salmon also carried out minor alterations on the main house. He had previously carried out alteration work at 172 Bath Street, Glasgow, 1917, for Mrs Hogarth Pringle.

23. Salmon, J., 'The Editor's Holiday', in *The Quarterly*, Summer 1923, no. 6, p. 26.

24. Letters preserved in the Salmon Collection, RCAHMS.

PHILOSOPHY

1. Salmon, J., 'The Art of Building', in *The Scottish Architect*, February 1909, p. 39.

2. Salmon, J., 'The Art of Building — The Future Evolution of Architecture', in *The Scottish Architect*, March 1909, p. 63.

3. Salmon, J., 'The Art of Bulding', in *The Scottish Architect*, February 1909, p. 39.

4. *Ibid.*, p. 40.

5. *Ibid.*

6. *Ibid.*

7. *Ibid.*

8. *Ibid.*, p. 39.

9. *Ibid.*

10. *Ibid.*

11. Salmon, J., 'The Decoration of Steel and Reinforced Concrete Structures', in *The Builder's Journal*, 25 March 1908, p. 272.

12. Ruskin, J., *Modern Painters*, George Allen, reprint 1897, vol. 2, p. 4.

13. Ruskin, J., *Stones of Venice*, vol. 1, Ch. 2, par. 17. See also Ruskin, J., *Modern Painters*, vol. II, Ch. IV, p. 33, 'Of False Opinions Held Concerning Beauty'.

14. Scott, G. G., in Robertson, P., *op. cit.* p. 181.

15. Salmon, J., 'The Decoration of Steel and Reinforced Concrete Structures', *op. cit.* p. 269.

16. Salmon, J., *The Scottish Architect*, February 1909, p. 39.

17. Salmon, J., *The Scottish Architect*, March 1909, p. 63.

18. Salmon, J., *The Scottish Architect*, February 1909, p. 39. See also C. R. Mackintosh in Robertson, P., *op. cit.*, p. 210, 'Science discovers. Art creates', and Vitruvius, *The Ten Books of Architecture*, Bk. I, Ch. I, pt. 3, 'in architecture, there are these two things - the thing signified, and that which gives it its significance' (Dover 1960).

19. Salmon, J., *The Scottish Architect*, March 1909, p. 63.

20. *Ibid.*

21. Wilde, O., quoted in Worsdall, F., *A Glasgow Keek Show*, Richard Drew Publishing, 1981, p. 52 (ref. from *Glasgow Herald*, 22 December 1884).

22. Lethaby, W. R., *Architecture, Nature and Magic*, Duckworth, London, 1956 (1928), p. 40.

23. Semper, G., quoted in Pevsner, N., *Some Architectural Writers of the Nineteenth Century*, Clarendon Press, Oxford, 1972, p. 260. Gottfried Semper (1803-1879) criticised designs which copied the physical appearances of earlier buildings claiming they resulted in 'Valhalla à la Parthenon', *ibid*, p. 254. Semper also recognised that style was modified not only 'by materials and tools [but] also by place, climate, age [and] customs', *ibid*, p. 259.

24. Mackintosh, C. R., quoted in Robertson, P., *op. cit.*, p. 207.

25. Kandinsky, W., *Concerning the spiritual in Art*, originally published 1914, Dover republished 1977, p. 1.

26. Mackintosh, C. R., quoted in Robertson, P., *op. cit.*, pp. 203-4 (see Note 22 — from Lethaby, W. R.).

27. Sullivan, L., 'Natural Thinking: A Study in Democracy', 1905, in Morrison, H., *Louis Sullivan*, (first published 1930), reprint W. W. Norton & Co. Inc., N.Y., 1998, p. 207. See also Morrison pp. 206-9.

28. Salmon, J., *op. cit.*, Feb 1909, p. 40.

ARCHITECTURAL ANALYSIS:
THE EARLY WORKS: OF ARCHITECTURE AND SCULPTURE

1. Salmon had worked on these offices during his apprenticeship in Leiper's office. See previous chapter 1888-1895: Youth and Training.

2. The project was begun in 1894 prior to James's return to the family firm in Spring 1895, but was not completed until 1896. James notes working on the building's interior in his RIBA Statement Paper of 1906. It is feasible the building was worked on in two periods. Drawings held by RCAHMS are dated March 1894 and note Forrest Salmon as the architect, as does a commemorative bronze plaque on the north elevation. However the signatory ogee crown suggests the younger men's influence.

3. Mackintosh repeated the forms for his adjacent *Daily Record* Office of 1900-01.

4. Internally the original cornice work, linings and decorative features have been substantially removed over the years. The little that does remain does not suggest any significant stylistic development.

5. *The Builder*, 9 July 1898, p. 24.

6. *Ibid.*

7. William Leiper — from the Proposer's Statement for Salmon's RIBA nomination papers, 6 September 1906.

8. Author's interview with Mary Newbery Sturrock, March 1982.

9. The owners Mr and Mrs H. Lester advised that the carving work was reputed to have been executed by Salmon — Mr Lester's father bought Rowntreehill from the Salmon family in 1914 and he has lived in the house his entire life — interview July 1999. Unfinished figures at the [vertical] balustrades to the attic level stairwell suggest an ongoing domestic project and Salmon is known to have been trained in timber-working and the study of sculpture. Mr Lester's father commissioned James Miller to carry out minor alteration work in 1914, involving the addition of attic dormers and a single-storey cloakroom, which were all very sympathetically handled.

10. The windows to the lightwell are plain but for an arched head and perimeter roll-moulding formed in the render.

11. Francis Derwent Wood (1871-1926) was born in Keswick on 15 October 1871 and educated in Lausanne and at the School of Art, Karlsruhe, Germany. He studied with Lantièri at the RCA in 1889, and assisted both Legros — friend and classmate of Rodin — at the Slade School during 1890-92, and Brock in 1894. Before becoming modeling master at the Glasgow School of Art in 1897, he worked in Paris. Through the Glasgow School of Art he met William Forrest Salmon and James Salmon and remained in Glasgow until 1901.

12. *The Architect,* 24 April 1903, p. 279.

13. *Building Industries,* 16 October 1915, p. 109.

14. Ruskin, J., 'Lectures on Painting and Architecture', New York United States Book Co., reprint 1897, p. 277.

15. Wittkower, R., *Sculpture,* Allen Lane, London, 1977, p. 102.

16. *Ibid.*

17. *Ibid,* p. 116.

18. As previously noted William Leiper, Salmon's master, used Michaelangelo's Medici Chapel images on the Sun Life Insurance Offices.

19. Rodin, A., quoted in Elsen, A. E., *Rodin,* Secker & Walberg, London, 1974, p. 138.

20. Elsen, A. E., *op.cit.,* p. 188.

21. *Ibid.*

22. *Ibid.*

23. Rodin generally considered the surface as the 'Extremity of a volume, instead of visualising the different parts of the body as more or less plane surfaces, I imagined them to be projections of internal volumes ... Thus the truth of my figures: instead of being superficial (on the surface only) they seem to grow from inside out, just as life itself.' — quoted in Wittkower, R., *op cit.,* p. 240. Interestingly Kenneth Frampton has also noted that Louis Sullivan, 'inspired by Nietzsche, regarded his buildings as emanations of some eternal force', *Modern Architecture,* p. 56.

24. Salmon, J., 'The Decoration of Steel and Reinforced Concrete Structures', in *The Builder's Journal and Architectural Engineer,* 25 March 1908, p. 272.
These comments were actually made in regard to concrete but reveal his general awareness of the effects on form of material and surface treatment. He also later lectured students of the Glasgow School of Art specifically on architecture and sculpture: see *Building Industries,* 17 May 1910, and *The Architects' & Builders' Journal,* 11 May 1910.

25. Although Salmon did not execute the sculpture many sculptors, including Rodin, entrusted much of the physical carving work for their figures to assistants known as 'praticièns'.

26. Ruskin, J., *op. cit.,* p. 273.

27. Sullivan, L., 'The Tall Office Building Artistically Considered', in *Lippincotts,* vol. 57, March 1896.

28. Mackintosh, C. R., in Robertson, P., *Charles Rennie Mackintosh: the Architectural Papers,* University of Glasgow and White Cockade Publishing, 1990, p. 186.

29. *The Studio,* Vol. 27, 1903, pp. 107-8.

30. Another similarly 'sited' example can be seen at 188-92 St Vincent Street, 1897, by Frank Burnet & Boston. As at 'The Hatrack' the pavement slopes and the building is set back, but the base incorporates less glass and the carving is more akin to J. J. Burnet and Edwardian Baroque.

31. The Roost, 59 Dumbarton Road, Glasgow, 1900 (noted earlier), by J. H. Craigie has features treated with a similar freedom as though constructed of a molten material.

32. Other trainees included Vernon Constable 1900-04, and Charles Alfred Harding 1904-08. Data courtesy of D. M. Walker.

ARCHITECTURAL ANALYSIS:
SALMON AND GILLESPIE: A DIFFERENCE IN TASTES

1. *The Studio,* Vol. 34, 1905, p. 56.

2. *Ibid.*

3. *Ibid.*

4. *Ibid.* The firm extended the building substantially in 1900, but subsequent alterations have removed many of the original interior linings. Remaining details include the entrance area wall paneling, stair newel post and balusters, and carved figures at the rear stair spine walls.

5. Keller became modeling director at the Art School *c.*1900 and gave lectures to architecture students.

6. Similar to that used at the Clydesdale Bank, 91 Buchanan Street, 1896, by George Washington Browne, where the stone moulding appears to pass through the flanking vertical stone brackets.

7. Walker, D. M., 'The Partnership of James Salmon and John Gaff Gillespie', in Service, A., *Edwardian Architecture and Its Origins,* Architectural Press, London, 1975, p. 242.

8. Archive photographs of the interior (after abandonment) have recently been traced in the Frank Worsdall Collection, Glasgow City Archives, Mitchell Library, Glasgow.

9. The multi-layered faceting of the peripheral 'rings' recalls the ironwork of 'The Hatrack' stairway and the section of a plant bulb or onion. Robert Venturi has linked the similar concept of multi framed doors in Gothic porches and at Karnak to the generic idea of nests of wooden dolls or eggs.

10. The work on the house appears to have been executed at two different times between 1898-99 and 1902-03.

11. Basement converted to lounge bar and property substantially altered.

12. *The Art Journal,* October 1901, p. 275. Another design for the same exhibition noted in the article may also be by Salmon. Commissioned by Messrs Pettigrew & Stevens it took the form of a Moorish fantasy, gaily coloured with tiling 'in strong blue and vivid green so dear to Northern eyes', *Ibid.* p. 276. It also integrated alphabetical patterns in a swirling stylised script.

13. See the Salmon Collection, RCAHMS. Designed and patented by Salmon, the 'Aero Electrolier' items were made and supplied by The Scottish Guild of Handicraft, which had offices in Glasgow and Stirling.

14. *Building Industries,* 16 October 1915, p. 109.

ARCHITECTURAL ANALYSIS:
SIMPLICITY AND THE HOUSES

1. Walker, F. A., 'Six Villas by James Salmon', *Architectural History,* Vol. 25, 1982, p. 115. The clients, Mr & Mrs A. Scott Brown, named Miyanoshita after their honeymoon location in Japan.

2. House now divided and Salmon's extension known as Kohala.

3. RIBA Licenciate Application papers of William Alexander Kidd, 8 March 1911. Kidd's papers also note a house addition executed in Prestonpans, east of Edinburgh, 1904-06. This has recently been identified as Walford, Ormiston Place, and displays detail features similar to North Lodge.

4. Walker, F. A., *op. cit.,* p. 116.

5. Nicol, J., *Domestic Architecture in Scotland*, Daily Journal Offices, Aberdeen, 1908, pl. 58.

6. Ferguson's offices were in the recently completed Lion Chambers.

7. Although subsequent alterations compromised the geometrical purity, recent modifications by the present owner, (Mr J. Hamilton), have endeavoured to restore and reinforce Salmon's original design aims.

8. Walker, D. M., 'Salmon, Son, Grandson and Gillespie', in *Scottish Art Review*, Vol. X, no. 3, 1965, p. 29.

9. *Cf.* Hyndlee, Venlaw Road, Peebles, 1922 — noted previously.

10. *Vista*, April 1909. See also chapter 1913-1924: The Final Years.

ARCHITECTURAL ANALYSIS:
THE LION CHAMBERS: FROM ART NOUVEAU TO MODERNISM

1. Mouchel, L. G., 'Monolithic Constructions in Hennebique's Ferro Concrete', *RIBA Journal*, 1904-05, Vol. 12.

2. Hennebique had exhibited his work in Geneva and Paris and sent Louis Gustav Mouchel to Britain in 1895 to publicise its potential. Salmon and Gillespie were aware of the system as used by Archibald Leitch for Alley & McLellan's Sentinel Works in Polmadie, Glasgow, 1903. It is specifically referred to in the Dean of Guild drawings submitted for the Lion Chambers.

3. Kandinsky, W., *Concerning the Spiritual in Art*, Dover, 1977 reprint, p. 52 (originally published 1914).

4. 'A Reinforced Concrete Office Building', in *The Builder's Journal and Architectural Engineer — Concrete and Steel Supplement*, 30 January 1907, p. 12.

5. *Ibid.* p. 11.

6. Venturi, R., *Complexity and Contradiction in Architecture*, Museum of Modern Art, New York, 1981 reprint, p. 43.

7. *Ibid.* p. 44.

8. Contrast the lightness of this effect with the mass articulation of 'The Hatrack'. Salmon was also acutely aware of the practical issues raised by the creation of an extensive area of vertical glazing. To ensure that the maintenance and cleaning work could be carried out safely on the north elevation, he also incorporated a 'Palmer' travelling cradle into the design. A note on the Dean of Guild drawings advised that the cradle could be used as a fire escape in an emergency!

9. Salmon, J., 'The Decoration of Steel and Reinforced Concrete Structures', in *The Builder's Journal and Architectural Engineer*, 25 March 1908, p. 271, paper read to Glasgow Institute of Architects, 11 March 1908.

10. John Cameron's design for a ferro-concrete mansion, Tillycorthie, Aberdeenshire 1911-12, surpressed the expression of the construction behind a façade influenced by old Scots styling. The walls were also thicker, comprising two skins of concrete in an early form of cavity construction.

11. Salmon, J., 'The Decoration of Steel and Reinforced Concrete Structures', in *The Builder's Journal and Architectural Engineer*, *op.cit.,* p. 272.

12. *Ibid.*, p. 271. This could be a reference to the work of Gaudi in Barcelona, as Salmon is known to have visited Spain prior to 1906, and Gillespie visited both Spain and Morocco in 1905.

13. *Ibid.*

14. Mackintosh read a paper titled 'Scotch Baronial Architecture' to the Glasgow Architectural Association on 10 February 1891.

15. Salmon, J., 'The Art of Building — The Future Evolution of Architecture', in *The Scottish Architect*, March 1909, p. 63.

16. *Ibid.*

17. See Elzner, A. O., 'The First Concrete Skyscraper', in *The Architectural Record*, Vol. 15, June 1904.

18. Salmon, J., 'The Decoration of Steel and Reinforced Concrete Structures', *op. cit.,* p.272.

19. *Ibid.* p. 270.

20. *Ibid.*

21. *Ibid.,* p. 273.

22. *Ibid,* p. 270.

23. 'Ferro Concrete in Architecture', in *Ferro Concrete*, 1910, Vol. 2, no. 1, p. 7.

24. *Ibid.*

25. Mackintosh, C. R., in Robertson, P., *Charles Rennie Mackintosh: the Architectural Papers*, University of Glasgow and White Cockade Publishing, 1990, pp. 186-87.

26. *Ibid.,* p. 186.

27. *Ibid.,* p. 187.

28. Salmon, J., 'The Decoration of Steel and Reinforced Concrete Structures', *op. cit.,* p. 272.

29. *Ibid.,* p. 270.

30. *Ibid.*

31. The Lion Chambers is reported to be suffering from 'concrete cancer' but current indications are that it can be repaired and saved.

32. Walker, D. M., in Service, A., *Edwardian Architecture and Its Origins*, Architectural Press, London, 1975, p. 242.

33. 'Ferro Concrete Design for Shops and Offices', in *The British Architect*, 25 June 1909, p. 454.

34. Salmon, J., 'The Decoration of Steel and Reinforced Concrete Structures,' *op. cit.,* p.272.

CONCLUSION

1. Service, A., *Edwardian Architecture*, Thames and Hudson Ltd, 1977, p. 115.

2. *The Studio*, Vol. 27, 1903, p. 109.

3. Gavin Stamp noted the 'Tuscan simplicity' of the Art School eaves overhang and linked it to Burnet and consequently American example – ref. Stamp, G., 'Mackintosh, Burnet and Modernity', in *The Journal of the Architectural Heritage Society of Scotland - Architectural Heritage III - The Age of Mackintosh*, Edinburgh University Press, 1992, p. 17. The eaves to the Govan Cross Savings Bank is a closer source both formally and geographically and was terminated by elongated flanking chimneys which later became a characteristic of Burnet and Campbell. The Art School commenced on site in May 1898 with the east wing completed in late 1899.

4. Although the meaning of the symbolism remains obscure to us to date (along with the Celtic traditions which may have inspired their derivation), scholars such as Timothy Neat have begun to examine and unravel their mystery - see Neat, T., *Part Seen, Part Imagined*, Canongate Press Ltd, 1994.

5. Muthesius, H., *The English House*, Granada, London, 1979 translation (reprint of 1904 edition), p. 54.

6. *Ibid.*

7. A revised translation of Muthesius in the *Scottish Art Review*, 1968, Vol. XI, no. 4, p. 30 reads as follows: 'Their exteriors however tend to be sensational due to the over emphasis on visual impact.'

8. This also recalls Rodin's earlier noted observations regarding the significance of the surface as the 'Extremity of a volume'. See also note 23 in chapter The Early Works: Of Architecture and Sculpture.

9. Mackintosh, C. R., in Robertson, P., *Charles Rennie Mackintosh: the Architectural Papers,* University of Glasgow and White Cockade Publishing, 1990, p. 186.

10. *Ibid.*

11. One of the studio houses proposed was for Francis Derwent Wood who had moved to the Royal College of Art in London following his time in Glasgow.

12. Crawford, A., *Charles Rennie Mackintosh,* London, 1995, p. 182.

13. Salmon, J., 'The Decoration of Steel and Reinforced Concrete Structures', in *The Builder's Journal and Architectural Engineer*, 25 March 1908, p. 272.

14. Salmon, J., 'The Art of Building — The Future Evolution of Architecture', in *The Scottish Architect*, March 1909, p. 63.

15. Salmon, J., 'The Decoration of Steel and Reinforced Concrete Structures', *op. cit.,* p. 272.

ADDENDUM:
GILLESPIE, KIDD & COIA

1. Coia's contract detailed a four-year apprenticeship with a starting salary of £12 per annum paid monthly, rising by £3 increments each year. Ref. Glasgow City Archives, Frank Worsdall Collection, J. G. Gillespie, Letterbook vol. IV, 6 August 1915-13 November 1916.

2. See Glasgow City Archives, Frank Worsdall Collection, J. G. Gillespie, Letterbook vol. VIII, 22 June 1920-19 April 1921. Other architects designing ship interiors included James Miller (*S.S. Lusitania*), Robert Whyte (*S.S. Coronia, Carmania, Orsova, Orama,* and *S.Y. Jeannette*), and John MacLean Crawford who claimed to have completed 'over thirty first class passenger steamers' in his RIBA Nomination Statement (Robert Whyte trained in Leiper's office at the same time as Salmon).

3. Information on Gillespie's input was provided by the late Frank Worsdall who interviewed Jack Coia on a number of occasions. Submissions to the local Dean of Guild authority confirm that the design was developed over at least a four year period - probably longer - involving a number of revisions, one of which comprised detailed plans by L. G. Mouchel dated 3 August 1926. Although this date was some three months after Gillespie's death, one must consider the time involved in developing a design with a client, producing sketches, briefing a consultant, producing detail working drawings, and reviewing the consultant's proposals etc all prior to final approval. Gillespie, as senior partner and familiar with concrete construction, would have had an involvement in this preparation work.

4. Chequered bands had in fact been proposed for the Hope Street elevation of the Lion Chambers and, although not executed, suggest Gillespie's involvement in its design. The work also included an unsympathetic mansard attic extension to the Ca'd'Oro, which was removed during the 1980s.

LIST OF WORKS

Architectural projects, 1890-1924, by W. F. Salmon Architects; James Salmon & Son; Salmon, Son & Gillespie

1890-95: W. F. Salmon and John Gaff Gillespie

Whitehill Public School, Whitehill Street, Dennistoun, Glasgow, 1890.

Offices, 209 West George Street, Glasgow, 1890.

Clubhouse, Whitevale Bowling Club, Golfhill Drive, Dennistoun, 1891.

Alterations and additions to Alliance Church, Strone, Argyllshire, 1891 (included stained glass work by Stephen Adam).

Additions to Woodilee Asylum, Lenzie, 1891-92.

Alterations to Printing Shop, Higginbothams, Springfield Works, McNeil Street, Glasgow, 1892.

Alterations to Deaf and Dumb Institute, Prospecthill Road, Glasgow, 1892.

Additions to Gallowhill Mansion, Gallowhill, Paisley, 1892.

Competition Entry for Burgh Buildings, Clydebank, 1892.

Toilet additions to tenement, 3 Shaftesbury Street, Glasgow, 1892.

Holborn Sausages factory, Armour Street, Gallowgate, Glasgow, 1892-93.

Alterations to Wilson's store, Sauchiehall Street, Glasgow, c.1893.

Scotttish Temperance League Offices, Hope Street, Glasgow, 1893.

Additions to Broomhill Home for Incurables, Kirkintilloch, 1894.

Laundry, workshop and gymnasium buildings at Whitehill Public School, Whitehill Street, Dennistoun, Glasgow, 1894.

Offices and chimney 'stalk', Porteous &Crawford, 94 Elliot Street, Glasgow, 1894.

Workshop, George Sellars Dyer and Cleaner, 102 Port Dundas Road, Cowcaddens, Glasgow, 1894.

British Linen Company Bank, High Street, Glasgow, 1894.

Dennistoun Infant School (including Drill Hall and Workshop), Roslea Drive, Glasgow, 1895-96.

1895-1913: W. F. Salmon, James Salmon and John Gaff Gillespie

Temporary store, D. P. Menzies, 30 Bishop St, Glasgow, 1895.

West of Scotland Convalescent Seaside Homes, Dunoon, 1895 (extended 1907).

Nurses accomodation, Pitt Street/Bath Street, Glasgow, 1895 (for the Glasgow Sick Poor & Private Nursing Association).

Printworks Building, Higginbothams, Springfield Works, McNeil Street, Glasgow, 1895.

Marine Hotel, Troon, 1896-97 (extended 1900-02).

Mercantile Chambers, 53 Bothwell Street, Glasgow, 1896-98.

Competition design for Glasgow School of Art, Renfrew Street, 1896.

Alterations to rear classrooms, Deaf and Dumb Institute, Prospecthill Road, Glasgow, 1896.

Toilet additions to tenements, Rose Street, Gorbals, Glasgow, 1896.

Additional storey to workshop, Glasgow Rubber Works, Ruchill Street, Glasgow, 1896-97.

British Linen Bank, Govan Cross, Glasgow, 1897-98.

'Rowantreehill', Rowantreehill Road, Kilmacolm, Renfrewshire, 1898.

Village hall, Lochgoilhead, Argyllshire, 1898.

Extension and alteraton of 'Gowandean', Lochgoilhead, Argyllshire, c.1898 (for Ms W. Salmon).

Additions, Higginbothams, Springfield Works, McNeil Street, Glasgow, 1898.

Van shed and stables, J. & B. Stevenson, 19-21 Houldsworth Street, Glasgow, 1898.

St Andrews Free Church Hall, 685 Alexandra Parade, 1898-99.

St Vincent Chambers (also known as 'The Hatrack'), 142a-144 St Vincent Street, Glasgow, 1898-99.

Toilet additions to tenements, 27 Charlotte Street, Glasgow, 1899.

Basement foundation alterations to shop, James Morrison, 39-43 Union Street, Glasgow, 1899.

Competition entry for tenements, City Improvement Trust, High Street-Duke Street, Glasgow, 1899.

British Linen Bank, 162 Gorbals Street (originally Main Street, Gorbals), Glasgow, 1899-1900.

Glasgow Savings Bank, 752-56 Argyle Street, Anderston Cross, Glasgow, 1899-1900.

Semi-detached house block, 2-4 Kingspark Avenue, Glasgow, c.1900.

Alterations to townhouse, 22 Park Circus, Glasgow, 1900 (and 1902) (for Mr W. MacFarlane).

Townhouse, 12 University Gardens (originally no.11), Glasgow, 1900 (for Mrs M. Workman).

Competition entry for Eastern District Hospital, Duke Street, Glasgow, 1900.

Alterations to office, Singer Manufacturing Company, Kilbowie, Dumbartonshire, 1900.

Alterations to office, 79 West Regent Street, Glasgow, 1900-04.

Lloyd Morris Congregational Church, 155-197 Rutherglen Road, Glasgow, 1901.

Competition entry for Glasgow and West of Scotland Technical College, George Street, Glasgow, 1901.

Toilet additions to tenements, 40 Dale Street, Bridgeton, Glasgow, 1901.

Boys Home, Deaf and Dumb Institute, Prospecthill Road, Glasgow, 1901 (including alterations to Earn Cottage within the grounds of the Insititute).

Alterations to shop front, Singer Manufacturing Company, 39 and 41-43 Union Street Glasgow, 1901.

Competition entry for Public Library, Main Street, Rutherglen, Lanarkshire, 1902.

Competition entry for Newton Park School, Ayr, 1902.

Design for 'Village' Asylum, Woodilee Hospital, Lenzie, 1902.

Alterations to British Linen Bank, 110 Trongate, Glasgow, 1902-03.

Three-storey class extension, Whitehill Public School, Whitehill Street, Dennistoun, Glasgow, 1902-04.

Nurses Quarters and Pathological Unit, Woodilee Asylum, Lenzie, 1902-04.

Townhouse alterations to 14 and 15 Woodlands Terrace, Glasgow, 1902-04 (for Mr A. Cross MP).

Toilet additions to tenements, 37 Dale Street, Bridgeton, Glasgow, 1903.

Alterations, J. & B. Stevenson, Cranston Street, Glasgow, 1903.

Competition entry for Elgin Place Mission Halls, Dobbies Loan, Glasgow, 1903.

Chauffeur's house and garage, Gallowhill House, Gallowhill, Paisley, 1903.

Competition entry for Renfrew Parish Church, Glebe Street, Glasgow, 1903.

Competition entry for Municipal Buildings and Library, Cadzow Street, Hamilton, Lanarkshire, 1903.

Extension to British Linen Bank, 110 Queen Street, Glasgow, 1903.

Interior alterations to St Peter's Church, Brown Street, Glasgow, 1904.

'Miyanoshita', Porterfield Road, Kilmacolm, Renfrewshire, 1904 (for Mr A. Scott Brown).

Alterations to 'West Park House', Skelmorlie, Ayrshire, 1904 (for R. Hunter Craig MP).

Lanfine Cottage Hospital for Consumptives, Broomhill, Kirkintilloch, 1904.

Competition Entry for Kirkintilloch Municipal Buildings, Kirkintilloch, 1904.

Extension to 'Walford', Ormiston Place, Prestonpans, 1904-06.

The Lion Chambers, 170-72 Hope Street, Glasgow, 1904-06.

Extension and alterations to Catholic Apostolic Church, McAslin Street, Glasgow, 1905-06.

Alterations and extension to offices, 88 West Regent, Glasgow, 1905.

Competition entry for the Mitchell Library, North Street, Glasgow, 1905.

Workshop/studio, Wm. Nicol, Clincart Road, Mount Florida, Glasgow, 1905.

'Den O'Gryffe', off Knockbuckle Road, Kilmacolm, Renfrewshire, 1905-06 (for Mr R. M. Thorne — extended 1907 for Mr W. F. Lanchester).

Extension to 'Northernhay', Duchal Road, Kilmacolm, Renfrewshire, 1906 (for Mr T. Service). Extension now called 'Kohala'.

'North Lodge', Church Street, Edzell, Angus, 1905-06 (for Ms M. Alexander).

'Dilkush', Gryffe Road, Kilmacolm, Lanarkshire, 1906 (for Mr A. Crosbie Turner). Property now called 'Hazelhope'.

'Bolfrax', 224 Fenwick Road, Giffnock, Glasgow, 1906 (for Mr J. W. Milne).

Cartsburn Public School, Greenock, Renfrewshire, 1906-09.

Stable, Winton Drive, Giffnock, Glasgow, 1907 (for Mr J. Seymour).

'Nether Knockbuckle', off Florence Drive, Kilmacolm, Renfrewshire, 1907 (for Mr A. D. Ferguson). Property also known as 'Lademarge' at one time.

Competition entry for the Liberal Club, St George's Place, Glasgow, 1907.

Competition entry for London County Halls, Westminster Bridge-Belvedere Road, London, 1907.

Competition entry for Town Hall Building, Perth, 1907.

Alterations to kitchen, West of Scotland Convalescent Homes, Dunoon, 1907.

Ten workmen's cottages, Steel Company of Scotland, Garthamlock and Queenslie Colliery, near Shettleston, Glasgow, 1907-08.

Bakery, King Street, Stranraer, Galloway, 1908.

Alterations to British Linen Bank, 3-3A Hanover Street, Glasgow, 1908-09.

Tool house, shelter and landscaping/groundworks, Kilmacolm Golf Club, Porterfield Road, Kilmacolm, 1908 (golf course also modified at this time).

Alterations to Bakery, 19 Houldsworth Street, Glasgow, 1908 (altered again 1911 — both for J. & B. Stevenson, Cranstonhill Bakeries).

Competition entry for Cottage Hospital Blantyre, Blantyre, Lanarkshire, 1908.

Competition winning design for Stirling Municipal Buildings, Corn Exchange-King Street, Stirling, 1908 (executed by J. G. Gillespie 1915-18).

Alterations and additions to Industrial Shelter, Glasgow Charity Organisation Society, Killearn Street, Possilpark, Glasgow, 1908.

Competition entry for Municipal Offices of Glamorgan County Council, Glamorgan, 1908-09.

Competition entry for Hamilton Academy, Auchincampbell Road, Hamilton, Lanarkshire, 1909.

Competition entry to extend Rutherglen Town Hall, Rutherglen, 1909.

Competition entry for ferro-concrete shop and offices, 1909.

Co-ownership cottages, Broomknowe Road-Castlehill Road, Kilmacolm, 1909 (development by Salmon, Son & Gillespie).

Alterations to 'Auchendoune', Doune, Stirlingshire, 1909 (for Trustees of Charles De Neville).

Alterations to Alliance Assurance Company Offices, 151 West George Street, Glasgow, 1909 (light fittings by Scottish Guild of Handicrafts, Stirling).

Garden Suburb, Cove Farm, Gourock, 1909-10 (executed on reduced scale, 1916).

Alterations to offices, Ann Street-36 Oswald Street, 1910.

Fireplace design, 6 Cathedral Square, Glasgow, 1910 (for Dr James Devon).

Alterations to 'Ashfield', Central Avenue-Beech Avenue, Cambuslang, 1910 (for Mr J. T. T. Brown).

Offices of Steel Company of Scotland, Blochairn Road, Bolchairn, Glasgow, 1910-11.

Competition-winning design for new clubhouse, Pollok Golf Club, Pollok Estate, Pollokshaws, Glasgow, 1911 (executed by J. G. Gillespie c.1913).

Hearth and stained glass work, 15 Park Gardens South, Partick, Glasgow, 1911 (for P. M. Martin Esq.).

Decoration and heating installation, 'Drumlanrig', Newark Drive, Polloksheilds, Glasgow, 1911 (for J. Stevenson). Later work executed by J. G. Gillespie, 1915.

Bakery, Cranston Street, Glasgow, 1912 (for J. & B. Stevenson, Cranstonhill).

Hall and offices for United Free Church, London Road, Glasgow, 1912-13 (further alterations executed in 1914).

Electric lighting installation, 1 North Park Terrace, Glasgow, 1913 (for Dr J. Devon).

Projects by Salmon & Son & Gillespie not yet located:

Porch to 'Houghton', Kilmacolm, 1907-09 (for Mr Burnside Esq.).

Laundry to 'Vellore', Polmont, 1909.

British Linen Bank, Thurso, 1905.

British Linen Bank, Stromness, Orkney Islands, 1905.

British Linen Bank, Kirkwall, Orkney Islands, 1905.

1913-24: James Salmon

Motor garage and internal alterations, 1-3 Richmond Street, Glasgow, 1914 (for Dr J. Green).

Competition entry for Gourock Municipal Buildings, Gourock, 1914-15.

Competition entry for housing scheme, Roxburgh Street, Greenock, 1915.

Alterations to house and garden, and new garage, 'Hastings Lodge', 74 St Andrews Drive, Glasgow, 1915-16 (for Dr J. T. West).

Alterations to workshop, 135-139 Shuna Street, Glasgow, 1916 (for George McLellan and India Rubber Manufacturers).

Hostel, Isle of Flotta, Orkney, 1917 (for Scottish National Council of Y.M.C.A. — Admiralty Division).

Alterations, 172 Bath Street, Glasgow, 1917 (for J. Hogarth Pringle).

'Lantern Theatre', Pitt Street-Bothwell Street, Glasgow, c.1919 (sketch design).

Theatre, between Richard Street and St Vincent Street, Glasgow, c.1919 (sketch design).

Competition entry for war memorial, Campbeltown, Argyll, 1919.

Fireplace designs, 'The Cottage', Cherrybank, Station Road, Killearn, 1920 (for Professor Carl H. Browning).

Alterations and chauffeur's house, 'Hyndlee', Venlaw Road, Peebles, 1922.

House and garage above chauffeur's house, 'Hyndlee', Venlaw Road, Peebles, c.1922 (sketch design for Mr and Mrs Lerrimen).

Competition entry for offices of the *Chicago Tribune*, Chicago, USA, 1922.

Alterations to form District Hospital for Women, 'Redlands', Lancaster Crescent, Glasgow, 1922-23.

Drawings/watercolours/sketches held in the Salmon Collection of RCAHMS where full details of date(s), location(s), client(s) etc are unclear:

Villa, 'February 1896', possibly an early scheme for the family house in Kilmacolm. *RCAHMS SAL 7/1.*

Single-storey terraced cottage block comprising six properties, Eastfield, Cambuslang, Lanarkshire, 1915, sketch designs for Samuel Galley. *RCAHMS SAL 10/1-3.*

Two-storey semi-detached house block, Cambuslang Road, Cambuslang, Lanarkshire, 1915, sketch design. *RCAHMS SAL 11/1-2.*

Two-storey four-flat block, 1915, sketch design. *RCAHMS SAL 12/1-3.*

Two-storey semi-detached house block, sketch
design. *RCAHMS SAL 13/1.*
Two-storey house, Busby, Glasgow, 1922, sketch
design for W. K. Rodger, precise location
unknown. *RCAHMS SAL 14/1-2.*
Two-storey house for Mr and Mrs J. Hogarth
Pringle, location unknown, possibly Killearn,
sketch design. *SAL 16/1.*
Municipal office and bank, Shore Street, *c.*1900,
sketch design. *RCAHMS SAL 20/1.*
Municipal property, sketch design, possibly for
Cambuslang. *SAL 26/1-2.* The sketch
may be related to a proposal for the
Cambuslang Institute for which Salmon
prepared a site plan. *RCAHMS.*
Conversion of 'Roselle', to a Hospital, 1921,
sketch design, location unknown. *RCAHMS
SAL 29/1.*

*Projects alleged by J. R. Hindle in 1979 (original
advice from F. Worsdall) to be by Salmon and
Gillespie for which no confirmatory evidence
has been encountered to date:*
'The Grange', 33 Langside Drive, Glasgow, *c.*1899.
Houses at 21, 23, 25, and 29 Newlands Road,
Glasgow, *c.*1897.
New clubhouse, Newlands Bowling Club,
Langside Drive, Glasgow, *c.*1901. Noted as
'Langside Bowling Club' by Hindle.
Garden city design for Argyle Motor Company, 1907.
2-4 Kings Park Avenue, Glasgow, *c.*1900, (this was
Gillespie's own house, but was very plain in
design).

**Original Lectures/Papers/Articles by James
Salmon**

'Architects, Their Relaxation'. Paper read to the
Glasgow Architectural Association, 1 December
1896. Published in *The Builders' Journal and
Architectural Record,* 9 December 1896. Original
draft held in the Salmon Collection, RCAHMS.
'Young Age Pensions', signed *'Nom La Ssemaj'*
('James Salmon' in reverse). Dated February 1903.
Original draft held in the Salmon Collection,
RCAHMS.
Nomination Papers for Fellowship of RIBA. Dated 9
September 1906. Original papers held in the
British Architectural Library, RIBA, London.
'The Decoration of Steel and Reinforced Concrete
Structures'. Paper read to the Glasgow Institute of
Architects, 11 March 1908. Published in *The
Builder's Journal,* 25 March 1908.
Incomplete original draft held in the Salmon
Collection, RCAHMS.
'The Art of Building'. Paper read to Glasgow School
of Architecture Club, 5 February 1909.
Published in two parts in *The Scottish Architect,*
February 1909, and March 1909.
'To-MORROW'. Humorous verse dated 21 April
1910. Original draft held in the Salmon
Collection, RCAHMS.
'Modern Architecture and its Relations to Painting &
Sculpture'. Paper read to Glasgow School of
Architecture students, 25 April 1910. References
in: *The British Architect,* 6 May 1910; *The
Architects' and Builders' Journal,* 11 May 1910;
Building Industries, 17 May 1910. No copy of text
traced to date.
'Round Skye in a Motor Yacht'. Travelogue article
published in *The Motor World,* 18 August 1910.
'Men You Know'. Article on life and work of James
Salmon in *The Bailie,* 23 January 1918.
'A Tax Talk'. Letter to *Building Industries,* 16
November 1918.
'The First Three Books of The New Prophet –
Sillabauk'. Humorous observations, 16 November
1919. Original draft held in the Salmon
Collection, RCAHMS.
Travelogue of trip to Norway, August 1920.
Original notes held in the Salmon Collection,
RCAHMS.
Five typescripts prepared *c.*1920-21 held in the
Salmon Collection, RCAHMS:
a) 'To Jugo-Slavia (Autumn 1920)'
b) 'Beograd and Dr Katherine McPhail's Hospitals
for Refugee Children'
c) 'From Belgrade to Sarajevo by Ford'
d) 'The Serbian Language'
e) 'Ragusa or Dubrovnik'. This article was published
titled 'The Villa Bravaçiç', in *The Glasgow
Herald,* 22 December 1921.

'The Balkans Today'. Paper read to Glasgow Art
Club, 21 January 1921. Reference in *The Bailie,*
26 January 1921. Original draft held in the Salmon
Collection, RCAHMS.
'Mouse-Traps'. Article by Salmon on housing issues,
in the *Quarterly of IAS,* no. 2, 1922.
'American Architecture'. Review by Salmon of an
exhibition of recent buildings built in the USA, in
the *Quarterly of IAS,* no. 2, 1922.
'Adam's Arch'. Letter to *The Glasgow Herald,* 12
October 1922.
'The Editor's Holiday'. Article in the *Quarterly of
IAS,* no. 6, 1923.
Hughes T. H., and Lamborn E. A. C., 'Towns and
Town Planning-Ancient and Modern,' Oxford,
1923. Book review by Salmon in *Quarterly of IAS,*
no. 6, 1923.
'Octal System'. Paper on eight-digit binary system.
Date uncertain. Original draft held in the Salmon
Collection, RCAHMS.
'Design in Construction'. Paper read to the Glasgow
Architectural Association, 19 October 1897.
Reference to this paper is noted in *Building
Industries* 16 November 1897. The article contains
no text and does not make clear if James Salmon
or William Forrest Salmon read the paper.

BIBLIOGRAPHY AND REFERENCES

Published articles on James Salmon and his buildings:

Cusack P., 'Lion Chambers — A Glasgow Experiment', *Architectural History*, vol. 28, 1985.

Cusack P., 'Architects and the Reinforced Concrete Specialist in Britain 1905-08', *Architectural History*, vol. 29, 1986.

O'Donnell R., 'James Salmon Architecture from Sculpture', *CRM Society Newsletter*, no. 42, Winter 1985/86.

O'Donnell R., 'From Art Nouveau to Modernism', James Salmon 1873-1924 *Architectural Design*, vol. 56, no. 10/11, 1986.

O'Donnell R., 'Acquiring a Taste for Salmon', *RIBA Journal*, August, 1990.

Walker D. M., 'Salmon, Son, Grandson And Gillespie', *Scottish Art Review*, vol. X, no. 3, 1966.

Walker D. M., 'The Partnership of James Salmon and John Gaff Gillespie', in *Edwardian Architecture and its Origins*, ed Service A., 1975.

Walker F. A., 'Six Villas by James Salmon', *Architectural History*, vol. 25, 1982.

Unpublished studies and dissertations:

Calder I. E., 'Savings Bank Anderston', University of Strathclyde, DABS

Galashan P., 'James Salmon II — Art Nouveau Architect?', Glasgow School of Art

Gordon S., 'Mercantile Chambers', University of Strathclyde, DABS

Gray R., 'Lion Chambers', University of Strathclyde, DABS

Hindle J. R., 'Salmon Son and Gillespie', Glasgow School of Art

Mackintosh D., 'The Hatrack, 142a-144 St Vincent St, Glasgow', Open University (copy held in University of Strathclyde, DABS)

McCafferty H. G., 'James Salmon', University of Strathclyde, DABS

McGhie G. A., 'St Andrew's East Church', University of Strathclyde, DABS

O'Donnell R., 'A Case for Reappraisal', University of Strathclyde, DABS

O'Donnell R., 'The Life and Work of James Salmon', University of Strathclyde, DABS, M.Arch thesis

Russell G. B., 'British Linen Bank (Govan Cross)', University of Strathclyde, DABS

White S. L., '144-142 St Vincent Street', University of Strathclyde, DABS

Public records and private collections of unpublished material consulted:

Royal Commission on Ancient and Historical Monuments of Scotland, Edinburgh: General Collection, the Salmon Collection, (and accompanying text by Walker, D. W.)

Private letters and papers of the Francis Family, New Zealand

RIBA British Architectural Library

Mitchell Library Glasgow

Glasgow City Archives: General Collection, and Frank Worsdall Collection

Glasgow Art Club Library

Renfrew Burgh Archives, Paisley

University of Glasgow, Hunterian Art Gallery

Glasgow High School Reports (held in Glasgow City Archives)

Glasgow School of Art, Collection Glasgow School of Art, Prospectuses, Reports and Register of Students

Minute Books of the Glasgow Institute of Architects

Minute Books of the Institute of Scottish Architects (held by the RIAS)

Private Letter books of William Scott Morton & Co.

Minute Books of Kilmacolm Golf Club

Scottish National Council of YMCA — Annual Reports

Glasgow Museum and Art Gallery, Kelvingrove

HM Register House Edinburgh

INDEX